The Real and The True
The Digital Photography of Pedro Meyer

With essays by
Louis Kaplan, Pedro Meyer,
Alejandro Castellanos, and Douglas Cruickshank

New Riders

The Real and The True: The Digital Photography of Pedro Meyer

With essays by Louis Kaplan, Pedro Meyer, Alejandro Castellanos, and Douglas Cruickshank

New Riders
1249 Eighth Street
Berkeley, CA 94710
510/524-2178
800/283-9444
510/524-2221 (fax)

Find us on the Web at www.peachpit.com.
To report errors, please send a note to errata@peachpit.com

New Riders is an imprint of Peachpit, a division of Pearson Education.

Visit the ZoneZero Web site: **www.zonezero.com** · Write Pedro Meyer at: **pedromeyer@mac.com**

Editor: Douglas Cruickshank   **Copyeditor:** Doug Adrianson   **Indexer:** Karin Arrigoni
Senior Executive Editor: Marjorie Baer   **Compositor:** Kim Scott   **Cover Design:** Aren Howell and Charlene Charles-Will
Production Editor: Hilal Sala   **Prepress Coordinator:** Mimi Vitetta   **Interior Design:** Kim Scott

ISBN 0-321-26913-6

9 8 7 6 5 4 3 2 1

Printed and bound in the United States of America

To Raquel Tibol, who stills writes on her old Olivetti typewriter, and to Boris Rosen for his ever present wisdom.

Musicians, Dhaka,
Bangladesh, 2004.

Street Scene,
Old Dhaka,
Bangladesh,
2004.

Street Crossing, Old Dhaka, Bangladesh, 2004.

Wash Time, Old Dhaka, Bangladesh, 2004.

Eels, fish market,
Bangladesh, 2004.

Three Tailors, Dhaka, Bangladesh, 2004.

Friends, Dhaka, Bangladesh, 2004.

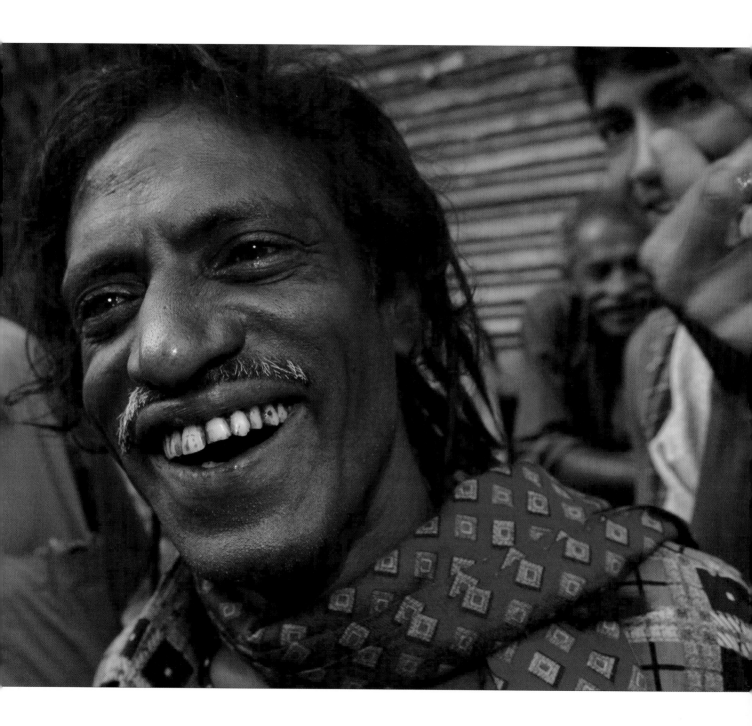

Liberation Day, Dhaka, Bangladesh, 2004.

Mother and Child, Dhaka, Bangladesh, 2004.

Buriganga River with Brick Factories in the Background, Dhaka, Bangladesh, 2004.

After School Hours, Dhaka, Bangladesh, 2004.

Movie Posters, Dhaka, Bangladesh, 2004.

Rickshaw Art, Dhaka, Bangladesh, 2004.

Shaving, Dhaka,
Bangladesh, 2004.

The Real and The True

The Digital Photography of Pedro Meyer

Acknowledgements

First I'd like to recognize Eugenia, Graciela, and Trisha, three great women, who contributed to making this journey lively and inspiring; and also Pablo, Manuel, Mauricio, and Julio, just for being who they are.

Marjorie Baer, Senior Executive Editor of Peachpit Press, made this book possible by first approaching me with the idea of creating it. My editor Douglas Cruickshank's persistence, patience, and thoroughness always led me in the right direction. If one person is responsible for any felicitous results in this book it would have to be Doug. I'm also grateful to Alejandro Castellanos, Louis Kaplan, and Ken Light for their important and insightful contributions. And I'm indebted to production editor Hilal Sala, designer Kim Scott, prepress coordinator Mimi Vitetta, and cover designers Aren Howell and Charlene Charles-Will for their painstaking design and production work, which contributed so much to creating this book. Benjamin Franco, our web master for ZoneZero, and a long time friend, has been invaluable in assisting me in making all of these projects a reality.

A dedicated group of people has worked with me at one time or another to make ZoneZero possible. They all have contributed in their own way to enable my ideas to turn into something real. Without their support none of this would have happened. I want to thank: Jonathan Reff, Pilar Perez, Enis Castellanos, Liliana Nieto del Rio, Fabian Hoffman, Paola Stefani, Nel Farell, Julie Donadieu, Jose Luis Bravo, Alberto Verjovsky, Rocio Vazquez, Pablo Miranda, Citlali Lara, Andrea Velazquez, Luz Maria Hernandez Velasco, Rodrigo Muñoz, Ehekaxiuhitl Hernandez, Scott Immerman, Mariana Gruener, Elizabeth Cuesta, Brenda Sanchez, Valeria Perez, Emilio Figueroa, Alberto Lemus, Gabriella Gomez-Mont, Oscar Garduño, Ana Maria Gonzalez, Jose Salvador Huerta, Armando Garcia, Irene Mendez, Lizbeth Perez, Evelyn Reyez, Luis Alberto Enriquez, Jose Antonio Rodriguez, Elizabeth Ruiz, Miguel Angel Santos, and Alejandro de la Huerta.

Contents

A Note about the Dating of Pedro Meyer's Photographs In this Book

Many of the photographs in this book show two dates at the end of the caption, as in this example: *The Storyteller*, Magdalena Jaltepec, Oaxaca, 1991/1992.

Meyer frequently dates his photographs in this manner to indicate images that he's altered in a way that may not be apparent to all viewers. The first date is the year in which the original photograph was taken. The second date is the year in which the image was altered using the computer.

For Meyer's own comments on this approach, see "Double Dating" on page 116.

Pedro Meyer: Becoming Photo-Digital

By Louis Kaplan

Isn't it about time that we come to terms with the fact that photographs have never been *the* truth about anything?

— PEDRO MEYER, 1997

LIKE MANY OF THE GREAT European photojournalists who were transplanted to the Americas on account of the rise of Fascism, and World War II, Pedro Meyer is an inheritor of that same legacy of cultural diaspora and intercontinental displacement. It was this contingent yet decisive moment that would destine him to become a leading figure in Latin American (and international) photography in the twentieth century. Born in Madrid in 1935 of recently displaced Jewish parents who fled Nazi Germany, young Pedro emigrated with them to Mexico in 1937 when they were expelled a second time during the Spanish Civil War, and thus he became a Mexican citizen at the age of 7. Meyer's special relationship with his parents would become the subject of his emotionally charged and groundbreaking CD-ROM *I Photograph to Remember* (1991).[1] He proudly recalls that it was "the first CD-ROM that had been published anywhere with continuous sound and images."[2] In this work, Meyer composes a poignant slide show of 100 documentary images while he narrates the personal saga of his father's and then his mother's struggles with cancer. Keying into the familial function of photographs and the intimacy of the personal snapshot, Meyer shares a heartfelt story of filial piety that pays tribute to his parents. Coming out of love and loss, the project exposes photography's inextricable linkage to mortality and finitude.

While Pedro Meyer has never consciously referenced Jewish cultural content as a major focus in his work, *I Photograph to Remember* unconsciously invokes a key aspect of Judaism that is embodied in the injunction to remember (in Hebrew, *zakhor*) and it transfers that commitment to the realm of photography. Rather than remembering his parents via Jewish ritual observance after their death in the reciting of the mourner's prayer known as the Kaddish, Meyer memorializes his beloved parents in the last days of their lives via

---

1. While the original CD-ROM on Voyager is long out of print, *I Photograph to Remember* has now been made available on the ZoneZero Web site. See http://www.zonezero.com/exposiciones/fotografos/fotografio/pag1.html
2. Pedro Meyer, "Editorial 7," ZoneZero (June 1997).

My Father Flying, 1987, from *I Photograph to Remember*, 1991.

photography so that the project functions in retrospect as a *memento mori* (literally, reminders of death). In this way, *I Photograph to Remember* is linked to both the memory of life and death.

Documentary Approaches

While Pedro Meyer founded the Photographic Art Group (Grupo Arte Fotográfico) in Mexico City in the mid 1960s, and showed his work in a variety of venues including the International Photography Fair in New York in 1966, it was not until 1974 that he left the world of industry to devote himself entirely to photography. Meyer soon moved to the forefront of Mexican and Latin American photography, not only as a producer of important documentary images but also as an institutional organizer. In 1977, Meyer founded and became the first president of Consejo Mexicano de Fotografía (Mexican Council of Photography) and, in 1978, he helped to organize the First Exhibition of Latin American Photography in conjunction with a major colloquium on the theme "What is and could be Latin American social photography?" In his historical survey, *Mexican Suite: A History of Photography in Mexico*, Olivier Debroise reviews these pivotal years of photographic institution-building and he quotes from Meyer's inaugural address to the second Latin American colloquium in 1981. "Those who seek to transplant foreign concerns and criteria to their new [and native] reality, in the name of the 'universality of art,' will almost surely find themselves feeling displaced and alienated."[3] Parallel to those critics who spoke against Edward Steichen's blockbuster photo exhibition *The Family of Man* as an attempt to whitewash

3. Olivier Debroise, *Mexican Suite: A History of Photography in Mexico* (Austin, TX: University of Texas Press, 2001), p. 7.

Above: *The Double Mask of Ocumichu*, Mexico, 1980.
Opposite: In 1978, Meyer was the first photographer to be allowed to document activities in the Sandinista training camps in Nicaragua.

particular cultural differences a generation earlier, Meyer sought to defend the photo-cultural particulars of contemporary Latin American life against those who would ignore or reduce such differences in the name of false universalist assertions that masked their own partial interests. It is also possible that Meyer made the plea for photographic authenticity ("of being true to oneself") in order to ward off the displacement and alienation that was part and parcel of his own personal life journey.

The type of work that Pedro Meyer produced in this period was very much in synch with his own call for the direct documentation of Mexican and Latin American social, political, and cultural realities. Thus, he cast an ironic gaze on the street life of Mexico City. As Debroise puts it, "Meyer then subjected the outside world to his intrusive glance, directing it at subjects he encountered in the streets and restaurants, at parties, nightclubs, and discotheques."[4] Meyer also traveled to Nicaragua in 1978 and became the first photographer to be allowed access to document the Sandinista training camps. But this period of Meyer's career was not without its provocations, and he offended many people with his piercing style of camerawork. That is why Debroise characterizes Meyer's street photography as "aggressive, irreverent, and even violent," and he underscores "his caustic nature, his genuine cruelty."[5]

4. Ibid., p. 153.
5. Olivier Debroise, *Mexican Suite: A History of Photography in Mexico* (Austin, TX: University of Texas Press, 2001), p. 154.

In response to Debroise's characterization of his work, Meyer asks, "What is this with being cruel? Is looking at the world with integrity an act of cruelty, or honesty? Isn't art supposed to allow a new look at the world, and with a different gaze, to learn from that which was not *seen* before? I believe Debroise's take on this matter is highly unsophisticated and lacking in any understanding of what I was doing."

While involved with numerous photography exhibitions and catalogues, Meyer did not publish a book-length publication in this intensive documentary period until the mid '80s. Interestingly enough, his first major anthology was published in Italy on the occasion of the cultural prize that he received from the City of Anghiari. Entitled *Tiempos de America* (*American Times*), the 1985 book consists of a "greatest hits" of his black-and-white documentary images, and it includes many photographs of Mexican religious festivals. This book was quickly followed by *Espejo de Espinas (Mirror of Thorns)* in 1986 and *Los Cohetes Duraron Todo el Dia (The Fireworks Lasted All Day)* in 1988. The latter documentary project was commissioned by Petroleos Mexicanos to examine the life of the oil worker.

Truths & Fictions: Across the Digital Divide

I Photograph to Remember, produced by the Voyager Company, was technologically innovative because it was an early CD-ROM and because these images were already shot as digital photographs. Contrary to the popular misconception that all digital images must be tampered with by necessity, those in *I Photograph to Remember* are not manipulated. In this way, these images function as documentary evidence and they are to be evaluated according to the conventions of traditional photography. But this lack of photo-manipulation was soon to change with *Truths & Fictions* (1995), a project that Meyer subtitled *A Journey from Documentary to Digital Photography*. Published as both a book and a CD-ROM, this was the groundbreaking project that was to transform Meyer into one of the leading proponents of digital photography. It clearly demonstrated the powerful impact that the computer and software imaging programs had on his vision of photography. Meyer's digital self-portrait on the back cover of the book *Pedro Meyer vs. The Death of Photography* (1991/1994) is an allegorical representation of this transformation. The photographer stages himself as breathing new life into the dead skeleton of documentary photography through the power of the digital imagination. In a visual pun, Meyer gives the nod to Apple as the maker of the preferred operating system that powers his mind's eye and that enables his magical digital montage manipulations.

Truths & Fictions is a book that straddles the border between the United States and Mexico and contains an equal share of color and black-and-white (mostly digital) photographs. Meyer's access to the "American way of life" increased when he was awarded a Guggenheim Fellowship in 1987 to photograph contemporary life in the United States. There are some parallels between Meyer's satirical and questioning look at America in the Reagan/Bush I era and the journey of the Swiss-Jewish émigré Robert Frank in the McCarthy-era mid '50s and the publication of *The Americans* (1955). However, there are also key differences in terms of both the new techniques and subject matter that are exhibited in *Truths & Fictions*. On the one hand, there is a great divide between the snapshot aesthetic of Frank's grainy

Pedro Meyer vs. The Death of Photography, 1991/1994.

Religious Syncretism, Santiago Nu Yoo, Oaxaca, 1990/1993.

The project also features approximately two dozen images originally made on a *National Geographic* assignment of the Mixtec peoples of the Oaxaca region of Mexico in which Meyer highlights their intense religiosity and the rituals of their indigenously inflected Christianity. In a digital montage such as *Religious Syncretism* Santiago Nu Yoo, Oaxaca, 1990/1993, Meyer juxtaposes a pre-Columbian statue in the foreground with the fragment of an arm of someone holding a basketball in front of what appears to be a Christian place of worship. Here, the secular god of "hoops" encounters the Christian church as well as a native religious deity.[6] While there are clearly economic differences north and south of the border, Meyer images the racial/ethnic, cultural and religious syncretism of Chicanos and Mexicans in terms of the concept of *mestizaje*. This describes the complex intermingling of European and indigenous peoples, histories, and cultures that has created the mixed races (mestizos) in the majority of Latin America today who cannot be assigned to any definite place of origin. In this way, *Truths & Fictions* produces a series of striking images of "digital Chicanos" or "digital mestizos" in a practice that brings technique and subject matter into dialogue with one other.[7] In the same way that the technical aspect of Meyer's digital manipulations foregrounds alterations, digital compositing, and mixing, these images illustrate the photographic representation of the mixed and altered identities of mestizo/Chicano cultures in the United States and Mexico. The technical emphasis on digital

black-and-white images and Meyer's polished digital montages made with the aid of the computer. On the other hand, Meyer was attuned to the demographic shifts and the changes in ethnic and racial composition that the United States had undergone in the space of those intervening 30 years so that it was no longer just a matter of black and white. As a result, many of the American images in *Truths & Fictions* focus on the (digital) documentation of Chicanos in California and in the southwestern United States.

6. This image becomes even more interesting, and trenchant, in light of the fact that games resembling basketball—played on a long court with a hoop and a rubber ball—were common across pre-Columbian Mesoamerica among the Maya, the Aztec, and the Olmec.
7. I take up these issues at greater length in "Digital Chicanos: Pedro Meyer, Truths & Fictions, and Border Theory" in my book *American Exposures: Photography and Community in the Twentieth Century* (Minneapolis, MN: University of Minnesota Press, 2005).

The Storyteller, Magdalena Jaltepec, Oaxaca, 1991/1992.

montage on the one hand, and on the other, the vision of Chicano and mestizo cultures in terms of ethnic and cultural mixings, makes for a project that risks fixed identity and that is openly constituted by cuts in terms of both form and content. With this emphasis on cuts and their openness to further alteration, the images of *Truths & Fictions* occupy an unstable and ever-shifting border. Meyer's "digital Chicanos" enact what the French philosopher Jean-Luc Nancy articulates when he writes that "a mestizo is someone who is on the border, on the very border of meaning."[8]

ZoneZero

In addition to taking images digitally and altering them into new realities in Photoshop, the visionary Meyer realized the amazing possibilities of the Internet as a medium for electronic communication and how it could become a digital photographic content provider. Thus, Meyer pioneered the potentialities of the World Wide Web for the exhibition and circulation of digital photography and for the interactive exchange of ideas about this nascent and emerging technology. Serving in the capacity of Web site editor of an online magazine and joining the ranks of the digerati, Pedro Meyer launched ZoneZero in September 1995 to record "the journey from analog to digital image making."[9] Within the very first year of the Web site, Meyer and his staff decided to make the site bilingual and to publish the magazine in both English and Spanish. This telling gesture replicated in the digital domain Meyer's position in the 1970s as the leading advocate of the value

of Latin American photography in predominately Spanish-speaking cultures and in resistance to the claims of the photographic dominance of "El Norte." This move also links up with the fifth point of ZoneZero's mission statement: "to serve as a bridge between creative minds from all parts of the world, but in particular coming from Latin America."[10]

In taking the name of ZoneZero, Meyer slyly alludes to a photo historical precedent that also demarcates the differences between the Zone System made famous by Ansel Adams and his own contemporary online project. Adams devised the Zone System in the late 1930s as a scientific means to translate visual impressions to photographic negatives and prints and in order to generate a regulatory system of photographic previsualization. Based on carving up the grayscale gradations of black-and-white tonal values, each zone represents the relationship of a subject's brightness to its density in the negative and to its corresponding tone in the final photographic print. Adams divided the grayscale into 11 zones ranging from Zone 0 (maximum black) to Zone X (pure white). In this way, Meyer's project makes the move from the analogical Zone System to the digital world of ZoneZero—from 11 graduated zones of photographic grain to the binary coding of computerized pixels (registering as either "one" or "zero"). As Meyer's first editorial states: "From the analog darkroom we are now moving to the digital one, where everything analog is transformed into digits represented through the infinite combinations of either zeros or ones."

---

8. Jean-Luc Nancy, "Cut Throat Sun," in Alfred Arteaga, ed. *An Other Tongue: Nation and Ethnicity in the Linguistic Borderlands* (Durham, NC: Duke University Press, 1994), pp. 113–123.
9. Pedro Meyer, "Editorial 1," ZoneZero (September 1995).
10. Ibid.

ZoneZero has become what many photo critics and photographers consider to be the most important online photography journal, gallery, and forum. A visit to the site (at www.zonezero.com) allows the user/viewer to navigate a variety of zones or sectors: Editorial, Gallery (featuring an array of curated online exhibitions), Portfolios (where photographers submit their own work in a forum that is free from editorial judgments), E-books (featuring ZoneZero editions that can be purchased and downloaded as PDFs for nominal fees), Magazine (featuring articles, essays, book reviews, and links to other recommended Web sites), in addition to a Digital Corner that contains reviews of cameras and printers. There is even a Feedback section that allows for a variety of interactive possibilities including online forums about specific topics, chats, and email. The newest feature is the Moblog section where ZoneZero users are invited to upload and publish the photographs that they have taken on their cellular telephones and thereby create a global "place of inspiration."

The impact of ZoneZero is not an easy thing to quantify, however it was named by NET magazine as one of the five best Web sites in the world in the area of the arts. Moreover, it is clear that it has created and sustained a large virtual community of the photographically interested on an international scale. In a recent article, Meyer emphasizes this networked aspect enabling photographic communication and a photographic community engaged in the ongoing activity of being exposed to each other. "I have made friends the world over, I have learned from people in countries that I hardly knew existed, and above all, the photographers who have shared their work with us in ZoneZero have all benefited from the experience by all sorts of exposure to their work."[11]

In the editorial pages, Pedro Meyer has done his digital advocacy work writing dozens of editorials with provocative and polemical titles like "'Hasta Luego Darkroom" (April 2001), "Why the Future (of Imaging) Is Digital" (May 2001) and "Redefining Documentary Photography" (April 2000). In this editorial capacity, Meyer has been outspoken in destabilizing "the myth of photographic truth" in any period of the medium's technological history. "Only now, with a heightened awareness brought on by the notions of what digital photography can accomplish, are we beginning to discover what photography was all along: the very act of deception."[12] In other words, the digitally wired Meyer now wants us to consider how manipulation and deception (whether in the chemical darkroom or in the computer software program) have been central to photographic practice from its very origins. Whether analogically or digitally produced, Meyer seeks to deconstruct the truth claims of photography. As he asks rhetorically in one editorial: "Isn't it about time that we come to terms with the fact that photographs have never been THE truth about anything?"[13] Here, Meyer reminds us of the tradition of combination printing, photomontage, and other darkroom manipulations that bred distrust in the photographic image even before the advent of the digital age.

11. Pedro Meyer, "Bridging Art and Technology at ZoneZero," in *The Digital Journalist*. See http://www.digitaljournalist.org/issue0203/meyer.htm.
12. Pedro Meyer, "The Renaissance of Photography," keynote address at the Society for Photographic Education Conference, Los Angeles, October 1, 1995. The lecture can be found online at http://zonezero.com/magazine/articles/meyer/03.html.
13. Pedro Meyer, "Editorial 7," ZoneZero (April 1997).

The Night of the Day of the Dead (Halloween in Hollywood), Los Angeles, California, 1990/1992.

Doubting Affirmations

In both his theory and his practice, Pedro Meyer's digital work forces a reconsideration of the truth value of photographic images and their assumed and assured reference to reality. The indexical linkage to the referent so crucial to the documentary tradition has been severed in Meyer's digital photographs. For Jonathan Green, they function as a new hybrid that he terms "documentary fictions."[14] On the other hand, Florian Rötzer claims that these are "fictive documents"[15] derived from a new computerized toy. But from either perspective, Meyer's images offer to the viewer artistic renderings that simulate documentary discourse.

In his introductory essay to *Truths & Fictions* entitled "Truths, Fictions, and Reasonable Doubts," the Spanish photographer and theorist Joan Fontcuberta acknowledges the unsettled and unsettling border that advances the technical implementation of the digital. He writes, "They are images that are situated in an ambiguous neutral space, as illusory as they are present: the *vrai-faux*, the space of uncertainty and invention—the most genuine category of contemporary sensibility. Today more than ever, the artist should reclaim the role of demiurge and seed doubt, destroy certainties, annihilate convictions, so that from the chaos that is generated, a new sensibility and awareness may be constructed."[16] Fontcuberta's astute understanding of Meyer's digital photographic work is closely aligned to what new media theorist Peter Lunenfeld has called the dubitative (doubt-ridden) processes of all digital media. In other words, the digital media are more closely aligned to painterly modes of rendering even if their products visually simulate the indexical signs of traditional photographic practice. This means that digital photographs are closer in character to the class of signs that the American philosopher of language Charles Saunders Peirce identified as *icons*. Peirce defined *icons* as likenesses that imitate reality but that do not necessarily have a direct physical connection to the thing they depict (like the classical photograph). Thus, digital photographs are to be viewed as imitations (icons) rather than as physical traces (indexes). Lunenfeld asks: "What has happened to this class of signs, and to the semiotics of the image in general, with the advent of digital photography? With electronic imaging, the digital photographic apparatus approaches what Hollis Frampton refers to as painting's dubitative processes: like the painter, the digital photographer 'fiddles around with the picture till it looks right.' Those who theorize this insertion into the realm of photography of the dubitative—which the OED defines as 'inclined or given to doubt'—have a number of directions in which to go."[17]

It is the foregrounding of this dubitative element (in terms of both technique and subject matter) that makes the work of Pedro Meyer in and after *Truths & Fictions* such an exemplary model

14. Jonathan Green, "Pedro Meyer's Documentary Fictions," in *Metamorphoses: Photography in the Electronic Age* (New York: Aperture, 1994), p. 34.
15. Florian Rötzer, "Re: Photography," in Hubertus von Amelunxen, ed., *Photography After Photography: Memory and Representation in the Digital Age* (Amsterdam: G + B Arts, 1996), p. 13.
16. Joan Fontcuberta, "Pedro Meyer: Truths, Fictions, and Reasonable Doubts," in *Truths & Fictions*, p. 13.
17. Peter Lunenfeld, "Digital Photography: Dubitative Images," in *Snap to Grid: A User's Guide to Digital Arts, Media, and Cultures* (Cambridge, MA: MIT. Press, 2000), p. 95.

for contemporary photography—a model for expanding the horizons of photography. For in Meyer's case, the epistemological doubt cast upon the digital image is matched by the doubt that is cast on the knowledge of what it means to be a Chicano or mestizo. This is the case with a festive image such as *The Night of the Day of the Dead* (*Halloween in Hollywood*), Los Angeles, California (1990/1992), which crosses digital masking (or not knowing what actually belongs to the original image) and Halloween masquerade (or not knowing how to locate these masked mestizos who live on the border). Working out of the cultural crossroads of Los Angeles, Meyer brings these two ritual celebrations north and south of the border (the American Halloween and the Mexican Day of the Dead) into photographic communication with one other.[18]

With the digital photography of Pedro Meyer, we enter a playful and magical world of alterations, transformations, and "becomings" that blur the borders of truth and fiction. This offers a reclaiming and a reformatting of the literal meaning of the word *photography*—the term coined by both the German astronomer Johann H. von Madler and the British scientist Sir John Herschel in 1839. As Meyer states in a recent editorial: "The word *photography*, as we all know, means 'writing with light.' ... To sit there in front of my computer screen, and to manipulate those pixels, has been the most direct experience I have ever had with the notion of what photography was always intended to be, at least from the standpoint of those who made up the word to describe the process called photography."[19] In this way, Meyer's "light writing" swerves its way toward a digital era of photography. This is an era that is inclined toward the affirmation of doubt, and one that puts traditional notions of "the real" and "the true" in visual quotation marks.

Louis Kaplan teaches history and theory of photography and new media in the Graduate Department of the History of Art at the University of Toronto, and he serves as the coordinator of the new Visual Culture and Communication Program at the University of Toronto at Mississauga. His book *American Exposures: Photography and Community in the Twentieth Century* will be published by the University of Minnesota Press in Fall 2005. It includes a chapter on the photography of Pedro Meyer.

18. This photograph is included with the photographer's audio commentary on the making of this altered image as an accompaniment to Pedro Meyer, "Editorial 18" ZoneZero (October 1999).
19. Pedro Meyer, "A photograph is a photograph is a photograph," (Editorial 61) ZoneZero, (October 2004).

Meyer: "I took the image of photographer Manuel Alvarez Bravo sitting in the chair when he was 75-years-old. When he was in his eighties, I took the photograph of him working with his Leica. I put together the final composite at the time of his 100th birthday anniversary in 2002. The image of the woman in the foreground, from Alvarez Bravo's famous picture *La Buena Fama Durmiendo (Good Reputation Sleeping)*, was taken by him in the 1930s. In essence, this image is about time, not the 'decisive moment.'"

Hand Reading,
Russia, 2001.

The Comrade,
Russia, 2001.

Ex-Comrade Stalin,
Russia, 2001.

Parakeet Man, Russia, 2001.

Russian Junk Food, Russia, 2001.

Monument to the Space Program, Russia, 2001.

Unknown Soldier, Russia, 2001.

Across the Street, Russia, 2001.

Oldest Synagogue, Russia, 2001.

Right: *The Redhead Red*, Russia, 2001.

Next page: *Monument to Lenin*, Russia, 2001.

ZoneZero Editorials

By Pedro Meyer

"Technology is content, and content is technology."

—PEDRO MEYER, 2005

THE ZONEZERO WEB SITE, with Pedro Meyer as its founder and editor, went online in September 1995 (at right is the introduction to the site that he wrote at the time). Meyer's first editorial for the ZoneZero site was published in January 1996. He continues to write these essays throughout the year and, as of this writing, has published more than 60. In this section, and several others that appear elsewhere in this book, a selection of Meyer's editorials are reprinted in chronological order, the earliest from the spring of 1997, the most recent from early 2005.

What you find in reading these short (and sometimes not so short) essays is the thought map of a vital artist, a man concerned with politics, aesthetics, technology, and the health of society at large; a distinctive voice—speaking in words and pictures—publicly grappling with ideas, both his own and others', as he explores and embraces a new way of working in a medium he took up decades ago.

Meyer is a man interested in questions and in questioning the status quo. One of the overarching themes in his editorials, and, indeed, in this book, is his questioning of presumptions about documentary photography. What constitutes fiction and nonfiction, and where exactly is the dividing line? What's real and what's true, he wonders. Is there a difference? In the world of ideas, perhaps questions are even more important than answers, and yet Meyer has no shortage of answers, and he defends his assertions vigorously.

Maybe he's right, maybe he's wrong, maybe he's both. More important, bless him for keeping the discussion alive in provocative, compelling fashion. At a time when many in the photographic community are engaging in the content vs. technology debate, Meyer embraces both, while challenging our assumptions as well as our perceptions.

—Douglas Cruickshank

What Is ZoneZero?

[September 1995, www. zonezero.com]

ZONEZERO IS DEDICATED to photography. Its name intends to be a metaphor for the journey from analog to digital image making. One of the references comes from "The Zone System," a fine example of the analog heritage in photography made so famous by Ansel Adams. From the analog darkroom we are now moving to the digital one, where everything analog is transformed into digits represented through the infinite combinations of either zeros or ones.

The name *ZoneZero* actually has several origins. It comes from combining the digital representation as in one-zero, plus the notion that the zero has to do with being at the very center—the starting point, if you will—from which new directions for photography will hopefully emanate. To use the words of the French poet Louis Aragon, in his preface to *Modern Mythology*, "Light is meaningful only in relation to darkness, and truth presupposes error. It is these mingled opposites which people our life, which make it pungent, intoxicating. We only exist in terms of conflict, in the zone where black and white clash." Hence ZoneZero

In conclusion, ZoneZero is a site on the Internet dedicated to photography and its journey from the analog to digital world. We hope that ZoneZero shall become a space where the following objectives will be achieved:

1. Every time you log off from this site you should be able to come away with a sense that it was worth your time and effort.

2. Any work shown here should have as its most important merit, not *how* it was done but *why*.

3. An ongoing debate on all the issues surrounding the "representation of reality" and other subjects relevant to the transition from analog to digital image making.

4. To promote the understanding of where, in the context of the digital age, the tradition of a "still image" is headed.

5. To serve as a bridge between creative minds from all parts of the world, but in particular coming from Latin America.

6. All services, advertising, or otherwise commercial aspects on this site must be, above all else, of significant worth to the visitor.

To these issues we will dedicate our energy and resources. We hope that over time we shall have accomplished such goals.

—Pedro Meyer

Who Has Manipulated What and When?

[April 1997, www.zonezero.com]

THE ISSUES SURROUNDING photographic representation are receiving increasing attention as the digital age moves forward. I have been asked repeatedly if I believe that digitally altered images should be marked with a special symbol to differentiate them from traditional images. My response has been that a symbol to show that a photograph has been digitally manipulated raises the question: What about all the nondigital images that have been manipulated?

Before I continue we should define the limits and parameters of what a "manipulated" image actually consists off. To think those issues through is already part of the answer.

In the end, what is everyone so scared of? Is it a matter of image credibility? And, if so, isn't it about time that we come to terms with the fact that photographs have never been *the* truth about anything?

Photographs are open-ended in their interpretation. I believe that is their beauty and mystery. A picture can have its meaning completely altered just by a caption. So, if photographs can't define themselves, but are dependent upon external factors, shouldn't we start to worry more about those external factors than we have up to now?

As photographers we all have endless stories of our images being cropped, presented in layouts to make an editorial point not in the images themselves, or of having our work edited out of context. What sort of symbol should those images carry?

I find the idea of placing a symbol next to a picture to indicate that it's been manipulated to be a simplistic solution to a complex issue—namely who has manipulated what and when? I suggest, on the other hand, that the more people are aware that photos have long been manipulated and still are—whether they're digital or not—the better off we'll be.

The Essence Will Remain the Same

[June 1997, www.zonezero.com]

HAD JUST FINISHED TAPING a temporary sound track in the living room of my house. It was done to evaluate how long it would take to complete the narration of the story for the CD-ROM *I Photograph to Remember*.

I was emotionally shattered from telling the story; after all, it was an account of the last years of my parents' lives. The idea of recording the tape yet again, in a professional sound studio, was something that I was not ready to deal with. For that reason the original sound track recorded in my living room became the final version.

The fact that the sound, which the viewer could listen to on that CD-ROM, was a warts-and-all version provided a quality of realism and integrity that was widely recognized as a real contribution to the overall presentation. My inability to retape the whole story turned out to be a blessing.

I found that having the sound—my voice—next to the images provided a very important layer of information that would have been missing in a printed version of the work. I don't say "missing"

in the obvious sense—that it was not there—but in regard to the emotional impact on the viewer if he or she hadn't been able to listen to my voice while looking at the pictures. Sound was not something that still photographers dealt with in the past; we were trained to see, not to hear. After all, the possible output for our still pictures, like in the silent movies, was a space without sound: images on paper, or prints on a wall.

The advent of CD-ROM technology, which enabled one to publish pictures alongside a sound track, changed all that forever. *I Photograph to Remember*, published in 1994 by Voyager, became the first CD-ROM with continuous sound and images, both digital.

Now photographers could create sound tracks that did not require access to highly complicated sound installations. It could be done with modest resources on personal computers.

We think that the time has come when still photographers will explore more and more the possibilities offered by having sound next to images. We believe that in the future, still pictures will be seen as either "silent" or "talking" pictures, much as in the movies. After all, we now have the technology to deliver and produce such options at very reasonable cost.

We feel that, from a technical perspective, there will be a convergence of digital still and video options, with both having access to sound tracks. In time we will have been as influenced by such new "cameras" as we were by the 35mm format in its time.

We believe this will provide photography with yet another new option with which to expand its storytelling potential.

As time moves on, the technologies available will surely provide us with more seamless and sophisticated delivery systems. But the essence will remain the same. Still pictures and sound have finally come together in a readily transportable medium.

Let Us Question the Critics

[August 1997, www.zonezero.com]

FOR ME, ONE INTERESTING development over the past few years has been the chasm between what the practitioners of digital photography experience and what their critics write about. I place myself on the side of the practitioners.

The critics often look at the work and say that digital photography looks the same as what has been done up to now, or they equate all of it with the "cut and paste" of earlier periods in art. On both counts they are wrong.

Let me elaborate, first, about the sameness to previous work. If I understand correctly, the critics' argument is that it "looks the same," but then what are we talking about? It looks the same as what? How can one say it looks the same, when one did not have a previous image to compare it with? So then one would have to imagine that the sameness is related to a generic understanding of what a photograph *looks like*. The expectation being, if there is such a big change in the medium it should be reflected in *different looking* work. Not an unreasonable assumption, I guess. Yet it doesn't reflect what is truly going on.

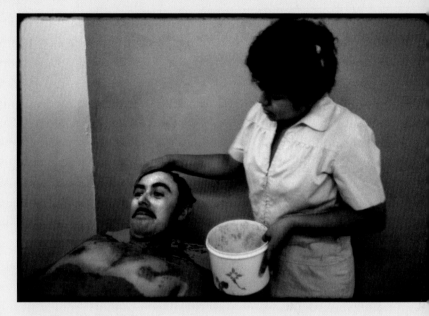

Mud Bath, from *The Oil Worker in Mexico* by Pedro Meyer, 1988.

How would a critic understand that I made an image that before could not exist? For instance, compressing time that would only live in a linear way within traditional photography. I can take time and play with it, representing events and situations within one image that only came together in my imagination, and from there moved to the digital format. This enormous change would not necessarily be related to a different aesthetic—as is expected—but in the understanding and the representation of time. No big deal? I think it is.

Champion of Checkers. "And I continue being the king. No one can win against me in the game of Chinese checkers during the after-lunch rest time at the Azcapotzalco refinery in Mexico City!" From *The Oil Worker in Mexico*, 1988.

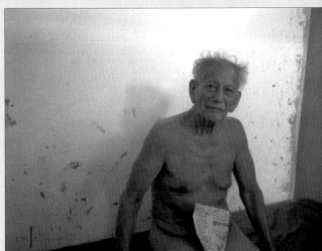

Yesterday's News Fig Leaf, from *The Oil Worker in Mexico*, 1988.

We are entering a period when the understanding of time and its nonlinearity is as fundamental to the way we live as any major concept that might have come our way within the world of art. We are finally in a position to go beyond that which was first suggested by Cubism.

People are no longer so sure if what I photographed actually existed, or if I brought together two or more diverse moments in time. Maybe the image looks *straight,* to use a very questionable adjective, but what does that picture then tell us about *time*? Maybe the critics have not given much thought to this issue because they are looking in the wrong place. Conceptually the photographic image has already entered into a new world, while our critics are still looking at the old model of construction.

Then we have the usually very simplistic understanding that we are looking at a cut-and-paste process, albeit a more sophisticated one. Again here the problem resides in the lack of experience that the critics have in understanding the scope of what these tools can accomplish. Describing them as more sophisticated is like describing a car as a more sophisticated horse. Yes, both car and horse will take you from here to there, but then a car can do so many things that a horse can't, which is why the car displaced the horse as a means of transportation.

Digital tools allow us to have control over what and how we can alter an image that was unimaginable in the era of analog photography. One quick example that comes to mind: the layering of images and the corresponding controls of each layer.

In the Mud, from *The Oil Worker in Mexico*, 1988.

Opposite: *Sepelio.* The burial of Florencio Torrest Tinajera, Reforma, Chiapas, from *The Oil Worker in Mexico*, 1988.

To try to replicate something like that with cut and paste is simply naive. One could go down a long list of other examples, but that would be entering a technical arena that would go beyond these few paragraphs. In the end it's not what the tools do that is so important, it's what is produced with them that counts.

In that respect, I'd say that the critics are not necessarily wrong when they state that there is no great abundance of interesting digital work in 1997. There isn't, but not for the reasons they suggest—that it isn't different enough from what has been done before. Also, "no great abundance" does not imply there isn't very good work out there already. After less than a decade in which digital image making has come into its own, it would be astounding if there were other results than the ones we—the artistic community—have today.

How long did it take for the critics to understand photography in the first place? And how long will it take for them to understand digital photography? We have to remember that critics have a pulpit from which they can make themselves heard, even though their assumptions may be wrong. Critics are usually not very modest in recognizing that even they have to undergo an intense period of retraining when writing about an art form they're not familiar with. Let's face it, these are very trying times and nothing can be left unquestioned, neither the pictures nor the critics.

The Mouse and the Milk

[November 1997, www.zonezero.com]

WHAT EXACTLY IS THE "third world" and where is it located? We know that sometimes it can be found in the midst of what are called "first world" cities, and at other moments it represents large sectors of the economy in developing nations. The term *developing nation* somehow implies that there exists a common denominator in this "development," when in fact we know that some sectors are as "advanced" as those in the industrialized world, while others are incipient in their economic growth. In fact there are no common denominators at all in this so-called development. There are no neat maps that establish where the "third" and "first" world realities start and end. At best there are approximations.

As we move forward in this digital era, and as communications media such as the Internet take center stage, economic issues become central to our understanding of what we are trying to accomplish. Photography is right there in the middle of all these questions. But let us look at photography within the larger picture. If you are reading this you already belong to that sector of people considered as the "first world," no matter where you're located.

Last week the financial markets around the world found themselves in a nosedive, where far and near had absolutely no relation to what was happening. While the markets in Hong Kong, Malaysia, Thailand, the Philippines, and South Korea had underlying reasons for such a turn of events, the repercussions did not stop at their doorsteps. Today all financial markets are interconnected by television news delivered by the likes of CNN, MSNBC, the Internet, and various other financial information networks. All this caused an instant world reaction and the markets dropped around the globe.

If we ever needed proof that news is now an instant, global affair, we need look no further than to observe what happened around the death of Princess Diana, or the collapse of the Asian financial markets. The reactions were instantaneous all over; there was no "third" or "first world" difference

Clash of Civilizations, Mitla, 1997.

in the speed of announcing these events or the response to them. This ought to tell us something with regard to the digital revolution.

But the fact that there was a worldwide response to the news does not suggest that all the people touched by such events actually participated in their consumption. Even though, in the case of the market declines, they will all suffer, many people don't have a clue what has transpired. We are living in a period where the people live not only in different time zones, but in different time realities within those time zones.

Some live in the digital era, but the majority live ignoring its existence—willingly or not—even though their destiny is being profoundly influenced by it. One can not extricate oneself from the digital era by wishing it away, any more than one could ignore the reality of the Cold War. Indeed, the ripple effect of the Cold War touched every human being no matter how distant they felt themselves to be from any direct involvement. I am thinking of a family of campesinos in Nicaragua; what did they know of the Cold War, yet no one would doubt that they were literally caught in its crossfire.

At ZoneZero we are reaching more people from all over the world in ways that would have been unthinkable only a few years ago. In the span of just 24 months we have gone from the equivalent of silent movies to spoken ones—an effort that took the movie industry decades to achieve was accomplished on the Internet in only two years.

With so many events transforming society at such great speed, one has to be cautious and observe how easy it is to be overtaken by events

and left behind without understanding what has happened.

This is particularly true in the field of photography. Much like the descent of the Asian financial markets, the market for photojournalistic imagery has seen a steady decline. In the advertising field, photographers who do not have the needed technology to produce digital imagery (altered or not) are increasingly losing clients. Teachers who do not have the needed knowledge in digital photography are finding it harder and harder to keep their positions, as students demand that their schools instruct them in the use of these new technologies. The 10,000 people at Kodak who have just been fired are yet another testimony that no one is immune to the changing realities brought about by the digital revolution. Not even Kodak.

The prices of digital cameras have come down rapidly and the quality has increased with each new generation. Computers cost less and less with increasingly higher performance ratios. Low-cost printers are now able to produce photographic-quality prints—an ability they simply did not have a scant five years ago. Film will be replaced with little PCMCIA cards the size of credit cards that will make its cost an almost irrelevant issue. Cameras that offer interchangeable options of moving and still imagery at high enough quality to be of serious use are already here. And still pictures that can be panned 360° are making the point of view of the photographer a moot issue. All of this and much more is what the digital era has in store for us.

Let's not forget that economic factors are driving all these transformations affecting the world of photography. And these same issues are also driving many of the cultural transformations that affect how and where photography can and will be used. Imagine the difference it will make teaching students photography in a poor neighborhood school where traditional film has been replaced with digital cameras and the cost of film is zero. Not a small issue. Imagine the students publishing their pictures on the Internet and sharing them with the rest of the world. Today, that is a real and practical possibility. Consider also the implications for the self-esteem of these youngsters. How will all of this make a difference for a child who grows up in this new digital era?

I am reminded of a letter John Berger wrote in *Le Monde* to Subcomandante Marcos in the jungle of Chiapas, Mexico. In the letter Berger quotes himself:

"In a letter written in prison in 1931, Antonio Gramsci told a story to his two sons, the younger one whom he would never be able to meet, due to his confinement. A little boy has gone to sleep with a glass of milk on the floor next to his bed. A mouse drinks the milk. Upon wakening the child sees the empty glass and starts to cry. So the mouse goes to the goat and asks for a little milk. The goat doesn't have any milk, it needs grass. The mouse goes to the field and there is no grass due to the drought. The mouse goes to the well but the well doesn't have water because it needs to be repaired. So the mouse goes to visit the mason but he doesn't have the needed stones to make the repairs. Then the mouse goes to the mountain and the mountain doesn't want to hear about anything, it appears like a skeleton since it has lost all its trees. In exchange for some stones, the mouse tells the mountain, the child when it grows up will plant some oak and pine trees on your mountainside. The mountain agrees and gives all the needed stones. Later the child had so much milk that it bathed in it. Later, as he became a man, he continued to plant trees. Now they hold back the erosion and the land has become fertile."

Is She Now Mine?

[June 1998, www.zonezero.com]

A **FEW YEARS AGO,** I received an e-mail from a Swedish student preparing his final report towards a degree in law school. He sent me a questionnaire on what he called the "balancing of interests in a typical sampling situation." He added: "I understand you work a lot with sampling pieces of old photographs in your work, and I'd like to get a feel for your attitude in this matter." He was obviously trying to establish what my criteria were around copyright issues from the perspective of an artist.

Here are a few of the questions he sent me followed by my answers.

Could you start by explaining the process by which you work? (How big are the sampled fragments that you use? Do you manipulate these fragments in any way?) What is the reason behind using this method? (Efficiency, making deliberate references, etc.) Do the legal aspects affect the way you work?

Let me start by explaining the difference between how I approach the issue of sampling and what others do. That difference is that in most of the images that I create with the computer I use my own photography, not pictures created by others. Having said that, if one takes the issue of the "original" to its full consequence, then one is faced with a lot of issues that have not yet been dealt with appropriately from a legal point of view by anyone.

For example, unless a particular image solely depicts a landscape (as in nature), most anything else contains man-made objects, which means that someone can lay claim to intellectual rights over the design of the objects seen in the image. For instance, most shopping malls in the United States stop you from taking pictures without specific permission precisely because the shopping center's owners lay claim to the copyright of all that is within their building. No longer is the shopping mall experience the equivalent of walking down your local Main Street, at least not in photographic terms.

However, in any traditional "street photograph" someone could claim that the building in the background was the creation of a certain architect; or a sculptor, if it happens to contain a piece of art; or the designer of the advertising in the

billboard; or the coat of the lady walking down the street; or the shoes; or the bus, car or tram; the chair; the clock, and so on—everything can always be related back to someone who created the objects that have been photographed.

Look at the photo of the two women in black walking down the street, taken by the world-renowned Henri Cartier-Bresson in Athens in 1953. It's clear that the strength of the image relies on the juxtaposition of the two women with the two sculptures on the balcony of the building in the background. It is obvious that such an image could not be created in today's climate, in which everyone makes all sorts of copyright claims.

If you want to explore this issue further, take any set of well-known pictures at random and see how many objects you can find in them that could conceivably be subject to copyright. It's astounding that we have made it this far without legal claims being made by everyone. One thing that is sure is that photography will never be the same from here on out.

Returning to my own work for a moment, I would say that the fragments I use within a picture have no relation to size; they are as large or small as needed, that is the only guide that matters to me. But that has to do with the fact that I am using solely my own photographs.

But let us explore another photograph made by Cartier-Bresson. This time the image is from Mexico, dated 1964. Here you have a little girl carrying a very large frame towards an opening in a fence. We don't know where the opening leads to. No question in my mind that the image is anchored on that framed picture. In other words, this would be considered in today's' jargon "an appropria-

tion." Yet no credit is given to the photographer who made the picture in the frame. Under present-day copyright interpretations, that might be considered a questionable practice.

In order to explore what the implications are, I have taken the example a step forward and brought the little girl carrying the frame into an image of my own.

The first question that comes up is what portion of the original Cartier-Bresson picture have I taken? Is it only the little girl behind the frame? Or is the frame with the "appropriated" picture also part of his original image? Because if one could argue that the framed picture is part of his image, then how does that play out with regard to my appropriation of the Cartier-Bresson picture? A second question, what is the amount of image that I took from his photo? Are the few pixels that represent only the image of the little girl, his? And if they are, then how many pixels can I take without being accused of copyright infringement? These are questions not unlike those that musicians have to ask themselves when dealing with music sampling: How many notes can be taken from someone's music without having it considered a misdeed?

Getting back to the question of manipulation, in your initial question you ask if one "introduces manipulation" at some point. Well, I see this issue very differently. I believe that manipulation exists at the very moment the original picture was made; everything else that follows are only ensuing stages of further manipulation. Art is about manipulation of matter and ideas, isn't it? And the final part of your first question is "Do legal aspects affect my work?" Surely they do. No one wants to find one's work facing a wall of legal issues. Think

©1954 Henri Cartier-Bresson.

The Girl with Frame,
1987/96.

of the implications for Henri Cartier-Bresson working today with all the copyright lawyers circling like sharks, seeing what they could scoop up to feed their hungry appetites.

Do you agree with the following statements? The original copyright holder should receive payment and credit for all use of his work, no matter how much is used and in what way. If it's worth copying, it's worth protecting.

You have to separate the issues of (1) illicit use that damages the pocketbook of the creator, (2) the reputations of the persons depicted in the image, and (3) the image maker who stood behind it. The issue of copyright goes far beyond just economic concerns.

I had a situation like this occur to me recently in Argentina, where a picture of my parents, taken from a magazine review of my CD-ROM disc about my parents' last days, was used to create a billboard that was plastered all over Buenos Aires, inviting the population to come to a rally in memory of an Argentinean policeman who had been murdered.

The picture of my parents was intended to portray the parents of this policeman who was killed. I had no desire to have the image of my parents associated with that repressive regime or, for that matter, with any police—especially not the Argentinean police, who were known for their fascist methods. So I sued the advertising agency that used this picture without my permission. A furor erupted all over Buenos Aires when the case was made public in the newspapers and magazines. It was an example of misuse of an image, which was lifted from a traditional source—a magazine—and the damage was not so much material as an affront to the memory of my parents. What price does that have?

It's interesting that, thanks to the advent of new technologies, many more people knew about this image and therefore were aware that someone was "stealing" it, and they were also aware that the picture was not taken off the CD-ROM, as many had suspected, but from a traditional medium, the printed page.

An American law professor wrote in 1991, "If a neutral observer can recognize the sampled parts, too much has probably been sampled, due to one or more of the following reasons: (A) He's taken too much (quantity); (B) the sampled parts are too significant (quality); (C) the public would assume that the copyright holder of the original photograph in some way authorized the new photograph." Are these reasons relevant? Is the criterion of the neutral observer recognizing the heritage of the sampled parts one that makes sense?

The law professor's statement reflects the traditional way of thinking—trying to establish how much one can get away with without breaking the law. I view this issue quite differently: It's like being "a little bit pregnant," you either are or you are not, there is no "little bit." And again, as with pregnancy, it can be either great or a disaster—it all depends. I can imagine having taken a lot from another picture, and it still being quite OK. The issue of how much was taken is not the sole means of determining what's acceptable.

Let me give you an example, which can turn the entire argument on its head. I could take the Mona Lisa image and then create a new image with that reference; there is no copyright on the Mona Lisa, it's in the public domain. But what would happen

Mona Lisa in the Wax Museum, San Francisco, California, 1986.

with the image I just created? Would I have no copyright protection for my new image because a substantial portion of my picture is derived from the Mona Lisa? Or, if my picture was copyrightable, would I then have by extension made the Mona Lisa my own? And if not, to what extent would that be true? The question remains: Is she now mine?

Let me introduce you to another of my own pictures with yet another Mona Lisa, this one taken at a wax museum in San Francisco.

Sure, the Mona Lisa depicted in the frame is a copy made by someone to provide the visitor of the wax museum with the illusion that you are there, witnessing the original Da Vinci in the act of his creation, but my image is nothing but the sum of these representations, which in turn have all their own creators, and so the spiral continues as to the question of what is the final resting point for this issue of "appropriations." It's interesting to note that most people imagine this picture to be the result of a composite done in the computer. The truth is that it's a "straight" picture, but with a much-layered reality. So, what is the difference if I do this in the computer or not?

At what point would you like to stop someone sampling your photographs? Would it make any difference if it were for an "artistic" photograph or an advertisement? Is the matter of "artistic integrity"—for instance, to be able to determine in what context your picture can be used—more important than getting paid for the right to use parts of your work?

A great Japanese master of ceramics famous for his breathtakingly beautiful teacups was asked if he did not object to the fact that there were so many lesser artists copying his work. He nodded, and commented that, on the contrary, he was pleased with that. In the future, when someone makes a splendid teacup, they will think it's mine, and all my mistakes will be attributed to those who made imitations of my work.

Aside from what this metaphor teaches us, I'd say that if someone uses some of my work and acknowledges the source, as I have done when I've used other people's work, then I have no problem with it. Probably, I would also want to see that my portion of the image would be a minor relative to his or her creation, and not its foundation.

Now, if the image was for a commercial use, I would want to know the exact details of the context. For instance, what responsibility do I have towards those depicted in my own images? Aside from the economic issues that would have to be dealt with, I have to retain the integrity of my own work. Today, you can see an actor that has been dead for a long time, John Wayne, appearing in a new commercial for beer. He might not have liked the idea of his image being used in such a context, yet someone is indeed exploiting him, and using digital technologies to do so. The same happened to Fred Astaire, who ended up in an advertising campaign for a vacuum cleaner, to the great consternation of many.

There are plenty of good motives to protect the integrity of the work that we are doing. Today, the possibility for unending alterations can be exploited by anyone without constraint. The need to protect the work with strong copyright laws is certainly justified. On the other hand, the mood for litigation can get so out of hand that the spirit of creativity can end up being stifled. It is our utmost desire that the child not be thrown out with the bathwater.

My final words to the Swedish student were to wish him well with his thesis, hoping that he might become a good new lawyer, with full understanding for the increasingly complex issues of representation in the digital age.

El Asombrado,
Ecuador, 1985.

The Dance of the Piglet, Ecuador, 1985.

Sun Dial, Ecuador, 1985.

The Rehearsal,
Ecuador, 1982.

Mystical Geometry II, Ecuador, 1982.

Bus Terminal, Ecuador, 2002.

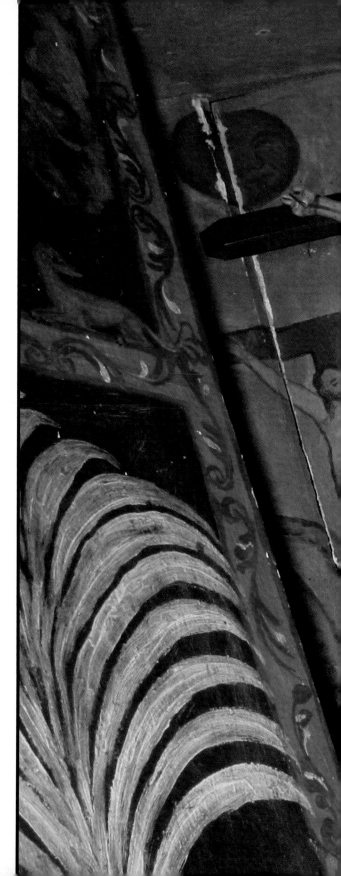

Saint Peter, Ecuador, 2002.

No son Limas, ni Limones,
Ecuador, 2002.

Kitchen of Ambato, Ecuador, 1982.

De Par en Par, Ecuador, 1985/2001.

Digital Critical Realism

By Alejandro Castellanos

Photography, before being a "decisive moment,"
constitutes a *series of decisions* that ultimately
converge in one representation.

— ALEJANDRO CASTELLANOS

Testimony, Memory, and Representation

In the 1970s, many Latin American youths, myself among them, were looking beyond the lecture halls and the communications media—which, generally, were hemmed in by demagoguery and an absence of critical thinking—for answers to the social contradictions we saw in the countries of this region. At that time, one of the few books that helped clarify Mexican reality was *The Night of Tlatelolco*, by Elena Poniatowska. It was based on the testimony of those who'd lived through one of the most transcendent social processes of the second half of the 20th century: the 1968 student movement that questioned the Mexican political system and launched the debate over the need to democratize our society. Sadly, the authoritarian response of the Mexican government resulted in a tragedy when snipers and army elements murdered an unknown number of people at a meeting in Tlatelolco on October 2, 1968.[1]

The cover of Poniatowska's book featured a symbolic image of the rebellion: a photograph of a festive group of students carrying a coffin representing the death of university autonomy, a principle often violated in those days by the repressive actions of the government. Through that photograph, and the others included in the book, many adolescents such as myself learned the value of ideas conveyed by images. But because of the dangerous circumstances at the time, the photographs were published without crediting the photographers who had taken them. Years later, on one of my visits to Pedro Meyer's studio, I realized that the photograph on the cover of *The Night of Tlatelolco* was his; to recognize it and to know at the same time who had taken it was a strange feeling due to the jumble of personal and social memories it evoked.

Meyer's print of the photograph provided more information than the one that appeared on Poniatowska's book cover, as the cover's format was vertical while Meyer's original was horizontal. The vertical view on the book cover omitted the

---

1. Elena Poniatowska, *The Night of Tlatelolco*. Mexico, ERA, 1971.

Left: The cover of *The Night of Tlatelolco*, by Elena Poniatowska, featuring a photograph by Pedro Meyer. The image was cropped by the book's publisher to omit the foreground, where a young man stands out, detached from the ebullience of his companions.

Top: Meyer's uncropped version of the photograph used on the cover of *The Night of Tlatelolco*.

photograph's foreground, where a young man stands out, detached from the ebullience of his companions, and concentrates on inhaling his cigarette. The man's ambiguous, aloof attitude contrasts markedly with the mood of most of the other people in the photograph, who look straight at the camera with conviction.

The obvious duality of these two situations—the detached man, the intense engaged crowd—was eliminated from the cover so that the image would conform with the editorial purpose. This sharply illustrates the reason that Meyer has insisted throughout his professional career on the necessity of overcoming our habitually complacent reaction to images. Doing so, Meyer asserts, will better position photography as a phenomenon in which the events it registers, along with the connections that emerge from them, form a dense structure that requires critical scrutiny if one is to comprehend its complexity.

As Meyer said in a 1986 interview at the time his show *The Others and Ourselves* opened at the Museum of Modern Art in Mexico City, "Photography is a lie that makes us see the truth; it is a lie when it goes beyond simple testimony, but it makes us see the truth because, moreover, it speaks creatively of the reality it records."[2]

By paraphrasing Picasso's well-known remark ("Art is a lie that makes us see the truth"), Meyer pointed out the key principle of his understanding of photography, at the very moment that it was be-coming possible to perceive the magnitude of the changes that made the 1980s a transition period for the medium. As a result, the concept of photographic realism, which up until then had been regarded as paradigmatic, entered its final crisis.[3]

The Others and Ourselves presented images of the United States contrasted with pictures of four Latin American countries—Cuba, Ecuador, Mexico, and Nicaragua—formally and thematically advancing an idea that Meyer used again a few years later in his show *Truths and Fictions*. In that exhibition he compared the social life of Mexico and the United States, and also deepened his critique of the truthfulness of photographs based on the possibilities offered by digitization. One of the first expositions composed entirely of digital reproductions, *Truths and Fictions* featured computers running interactive programs as a catalog in which Meyer and various authors discussed the impact of the new media on iconographic production.[4]

By using technology to link the creation and reproduction of paradigmatic photographic realism, Meyer took a position that was atypical in the Mexican context, characterized by a tradition in which the realism of photojournalists such as the Casasola family, Enrique Diaz, and Hector Garcia, or the metaphors created by Manuel and Lola Alvarez Bravo, Nacho Lopez, and Mariana Yampolsky by means of "direct" photographs, did not question the medium itself. Nevertheless, Meyer paradoxically accepted the possibility of

---

2. Angel Cosmos, *Conversation with Pedro Meyer*, in Fotozoom, May 1986, p. 15.

3. See the chapters "The Photograph Disturbs Itself" (1950–1980), and "The Photograph and New Contemporary Art," in Jean Claude Lemagny and Andre Rouille's *History of the Photograph*. Barcelona, Ediciones Martinez Roca, 1988.

4. Pedro Meyer, *Truths and Fictions*. "The Photograph's Journey from Documentary to Digital." Mexico, Aperture-Casa de las Imgenes, 1995.

Top: *The Temptation of the Angel*, 1991.
Bottom: *The Strolling Saint*, Nochistlan, Oaxaca, 1991/1992.

ideological and technological changes in photography from its testimonial use, a position that also distances him from those who, toward the end of the 20th century, experimentally explored the boundaries of photography in Mexico: Lourdes Grobet, Jan Hendrix, Carlos Jurado, Jesus Sanchez Uribe, and Gerardo Suter, among others.

Because of this, the images of Pedro Meyer open a broad vein for the reinterpretation of photography, which, from the beginning, taking advantage of his experience as a "documentary photographer," has provoked a crisis in the basic concepts of this practice. Meyer employs the very media that have caused several social documentary photographers to reject their use, arguing that the most important quality of photography is lost: its relation to reality. Meyer has cast his gaze elsewhere: image as knowledge, a solid position compared to the caprices of "the truth." Faced with these caprices, he sustains his work and its diffusion along three axes that allow him to emphasize and explain his perception of reality—testimonial function, memory as the repository of experience, and the critique of representation—thus offering to those who view his work a complex understanding of the photographic phenomenon.

Compromise and Fiction

Meyer's work is generally associated with a key moment in Latin America when the ideas of photographers from throughout the region underwent a maturation. This association is especially apt in the cases of Argentina, Mexico, and Venezuela, where various photographers not only dedicated themselves to creating images, but also to developing conditions in which diverse audiences could consider the complexity of thinking about such images outside the conventions of the prevailing media. The greatest result of this process was the celebration in 1978 of the First Latin American Colloquium of Photography, organized by the Consejo Mexicano de Fotografia (Mexican Council of Photography), which had been founded the previous year. This event, like its successor in 1981, was chaired by Meyer and helped to present—for the first time anywhere in the world—Latin American photography as a body of work with its own characteristics.

In a climate polarized by the effects of the Cold War in Latin America, which gave rise to authoritarian regimes in most of the region, Meyer defended the need for testimony as the foundation of the production of images, as is seen in his essay, *The Optics of a Latin American Photograph*,[5] published in 1981, in which he called for the creators of images to become conscious of their participation in the social life of nations, an idea that he revisited in organizing the Second Latin American Colloquium of Photography in Mexico City in 1982, which constituted an affirmation of principles, a stand taken in the face of social and political tensions.

Some of us, who were just getting started in photography in those years, took that declaration as an article of faith that did not allow us to think of the image as a territory open to experimentation or to individual reference points. Nevertheless, with the passing of the years, it is possible to

---

5. Pedro Meyer, "The Optics of a Latin American Photograph," in *Aspects of the Photograph in Mexico*, Rogelio Villarreal, editor. Mexico, Federacion Editorial Mexicana, 1981, pp. 71–85.

Nora Astorga, Sandinista Guerrilla, 1978.

recognize that the indicated testimonial function did not necessarily confine photography within the framework of conventional realism. Rather, by placing the social function of images at the center of the debate, it established a starting point for demonstrating that function's potential as a reference at the beginning of a new era of participation in Mexico's cultural arena.

For this reason it is best to distinguish the emergence of photography in the second half of the 1970s and the early '80s, when it was associated with a situation in which, as happens in all conflicts, wars in particular, many images produced in Latin America fulfilled informational and propagandistic functions, antagonistic aspects in an equation generally defined by the one-dimensional sense that is given to a photograph when it is regarded as a *document*—a word that does not fully describe the differences that Belgian critic Dirk Lauwaert has identified in relation to *compromise*, a term that usually accompanied artistic critiques in those years:

Meyer observes that the sign in *El Reverendo y Los Suyos*, taken in Yuma, Arizona, in 1985 (above right), "can be read not only as Jesus being a savior but also as an advertisement for a bank where Jesus saves. And the smiles of the deacon and his wife seem ironic when contrasted with the angry bark by the tiny dog. This photo could not be more of a counterpoint to *Algebra de La Passion*, taken in Ecuador in 1982 (above left), a man and woman reenacting the Passion of Christ. I especially like the blackboard behind them with its hand-drawn statement about the Passion of Christ surrounded by algebraic formulas."

"Here again," Meyer says, "we have the contrast between the U.S. and Latin American sensibilities. In *La Mona Lisa en Broadway* (above right), taken in 1985, we see a large, iconic image of the head of a woman, which is being used for purposes of commerce. In *Los Sarapes de la Virgen*, taken in La Villa, Mexico, in 1983 (above left), the woman's face painted on a wall references a religious figure, the Virgin of Guadalupe."

"These two photos provide yet another reference," Meyer says, "to the cultural differences between the United States and Latin America." *El Abrazo (The Hug)* was taken in Mexico in 1979 (above left). *Eye Bar* was made in Los Angeles in 1980 (above right). In Latin America physical contact is very much a part of the culture, whereas the opposite is true in the U.S."

The photos on the opposite page all appeared in *The Others and Ourselves*, Meyer's 1986 exhibition at the Museum of Modern Art, Mexico City.

"With compromise one takes a position; the document aspires to impartiality," Lauwaert wrote. "With compromise one chooses the process and the change (in the situation, but most of all in the observer); the document conducts an inventory. Compromise implies a time for change; the document assumes a place that can be juxtaposed. Compromise depends on histories, while the document trusts only the summary, the list. The document is an extension of the bureaucracy and its authority. The document places the subject in a position open to investigation and analysis, and thereby to manipulation and exploitation. Any aspect described in the usual terms of the document is condemned to alienation.

"The compromise, for its part, presupposes that the subject can avoid alienation. A kind of photographic liberation theology is professed by each compromised photograph."[6]

Pedro Meyer was an exceptional witness to a key moment in the contemporary history of Mexico. In photographing the 1968 student movement, he took a clear position for the first time as a compromised photographer, conscious of the testimonial value of photography in the political reconstruction of the events, especially when confronted with a regime virtually impervious to criticism.

Ten years after having made those images, Meyer traveled to Nicaragua to photograph the Sandinista revolution on assignment for the daily *unomásuno*, a Mexican newspaper that had emerged at that time as a result of the nascent opening in Mexican politics and whose readers were overwhelmingly students, workers, intellectuals, and leftist politicians who demanded information more trustworthy and critical than that offered by other media, which were almost always co-opted by the government. In this context, Meyer proved himself to be a remarkable journalist, not only taking photographs but also describing the revolutionary situation in articles and interviews. In this way he developed one of the ideas that had accompanied him since he first became a photographer: a consciousness of the limits of the image in describing complex situations. To relate his war experiences, Meyer was not only interested in presenting icons that would permit one to imagine what was happening, he was also intent on providing extensive details in order to give a more accurate view of the events, a position that led him to organize a show that was presented in Mexico, Cuba, and Venezuela in order to create a better understanding of the Sandinista movement.

Because of this, Nestor Garcia Canclini found in Meyer's Nicaraguan work an effective formula for communicating a historical moment: "An isolated photograph lacks narrative power, but a well-planned arrangement of a series of shots can show the dynamic complexity of a nascent revolution," in such a form that, "The photographer's struggle to be true to life, to capture synthetically social complexity, is today one of the areas where we can best ask ourselves what the function of art is. Where we can also allow historical conflicts to interrogate us."[7]

6. Dirk Lauwaert, "Document/Engagement," in *Positions, Attitudes, Actions: Social and Political Commitment in Photography*. The Foto Biennale Rotterdam/Nederlands Foto Instituut, 2000, p. 29.
7. Nestor Garcia Canclini, "What the Photograph Can Say About a Revolution," in Casa de las Americas, Nov.-Dec., 1978.

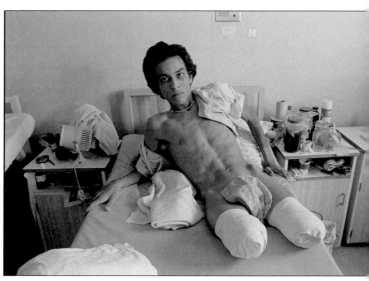

Somoza Destroyed, Managua, Nicaragua, 1979.

The Wounded Guerrilla, Nicaragua, 1979.

In the face of the close relationship between Meyer's intentions and leftist movements in Mexico and Nicaragua, two subsequent projects allow us to see from a different perspective the full reach of the image as a means of relating social processes. Both, moreover, are connected to the central institutions of the Mexican political system under the governance of the Institutional Revolutionary Party (PRI)—the presidency and corporatism—poles of the hegemony based on a dense web of symbols and associations that identified political culture in Mexico with fiction and deceit.

The course of the 1981 presidential campaign of Miguel de la Madrid, and the commemoration in 1988 of the oil expropriation—for which Meyer was commissioned to create a memoir and to edit a book—testify to the manner in which his "direct images" function in a context where reality and appearance constantly overlap one another, given the virtual nature of social and political processes whose complexity turns them into an enormous sham, a collective ritual where demagoguery restricts, on the one part, the critical possibilities of the image, generating, in turn, fictions whose resemblance to real life acquires an affirmative or rapturous resemblance to the national myths.

Both works take place in circumstances representative of any project that falls somewhere between an assignment and a personal observation.

Opposite: *Environmental Cleanup*, 1987/1988.

As often happens with photojournalists who seek to preserve their independence by covering events from different angles, Meyer gave himself over to the task of taking a position on events well outside his assignment—in one case reporting on the contradictions in the relations of the campesinos and the urban population with the candidate—who might as well have been the only candidate, given that he was hand-picked by the outgoing president, though he gave the appearance of competing for the poplar vote. In another case, by describing the living conditions of workers at Petroleos Mexicanos, Meyer committed himself to conveying the paradox of a celebration, which, if it affirmed the nation's possession and exploitation of hydrocarbons, also reflected the unfavorable situation of workers within the framework of a ossified labor and state bureaucracy.

From the Moment to the Process

One of Pedro Meyer's first conscious contacts with photography was in the pages of *National Geographic*. As a boy, his mother would allow him to stay up late while she read to him from it. Meyer has also referred to the way in which—as a child—the reflections of dust that light produced represented a lasting mystery of fleeting brilliance that he was able to capture years later when he photographed the phenomenon. The resulting images permitted him to "recognize the power of the medium to isolate and contain time."

A subtle but consistent simultaneity relates those experiences to the way in which Meyer has linked photography with memory, taking the intimate level to the collective, and complementing the close connection between the image and society that characterizes other parts of his work. He knows that the gradual decrease of references that the passage of time entails has in photography a means for resisting oblivion and expressing the emotions and affections with the paradoxical authority that in this case means loss. Perhaps for this reason one of the forms that he has developed most is portraiture: In the likenesses of others he has found a territory that allows him to explore and explain his understanding of human relations, departing from the qualities of the imprint, verisimilitude, and the record of time that are implicit in any photograph.

Because of this, upon learning of the inexorable illness that would eventually take his parents' lives, Meyer reacted with the expectation that photography would help him find a way to mourn that would allow him to remember his last days with them. Before his *Fotografio para Recorder* (*I Photograph to Remember*)—the final title for the work that resulted in a CD-ROM[8]—he had only referred to his personal life in one completely different image: *The Lady and her Servants* (1977), in which he had his mother pose with the household workers. The photo is emblematic of the relations of power and self-criticism in Meyer's social class—a rare work in a country where the representation of the ruling classes is typically obscured by the way they are depicted in the print media. The ironic complicity of that self-representation acquired many different, tragic, facets in view of his parents' illnesses, seen with a closeness that only comes with familiarity.

8. Pedro Meyer, *I Photograph to Remember*. New York, Voyager, 1991.

The Lady and Her Servants, 1977.

One aspect turned out to be crucial in the production of *I Photograph to Remember*: the impossibility of fully recovering the memory of experience through images. This led Meyer to take up a practice that he had not used since he created the audiovisual *A Sunday in Chapultepec* (1965), in which a panorama unfolds of the activities that take place every weekend in Mexico City's most popular park.[9] In the same way that the music and sequence of images in *A Sunday in Chapultepec* helped him to express a story that matched the experience in *I Photograph to Remember*, Meyer used digital media to compose a narration in which the image and the sound complement one another to form an integrated whole that elevates his parents' story to a universal plane—in the same way that autobiographical works succeed in transcending the individual anecdote.

9. To produce this audiovisual, one of the first in Mexico, Pedro Meyer designed a system that allowed him to synchronize the advance of the slides with the sound. The quality of this work won him a prize awarded by the Leitz Company, which presented the work at the International Photographic Fair in New York in 1966.

Opposite: *Fruits of the Sea*, Juchitan, Mexico, 1983.

In this case, the enrichment of photography's possibilities by digitizing reinforces memory, leading the observer to identify, or *remember*, the narration and its content in a way that can't be achieved with any other combination of media. But working with a single image—a self-portrait done in 2002, *The Meyers*—has become an emblem of his work. *The Meyers* portrays time in a particular manner that flows in circles around the four people who appear in the image. In fact, those four people are three, as Pedro Meyer is depicted at two different periods in his life: as a 5-year-old child, in a portrait with his father; and as an adult with his 5-year-old son Julio. Thanks to the possibilities of digitization, Meyer brought together the two different periods, creating an allegory of the way in which the new technologies affect the understanding of photographic time, which was previously associated with a single instant.

The basis of any digital formula is a binary structure, whose combinations make it possible to record and interpret the elements of reality in order to transform them into information capable of being transported at great speed along multiple trajectories and to be presented in the most diverse configurations. In this ambience, which entails a new crossroad of the technical image, Pedro Meyer has proposed to reaffirm that photography, before being a "decisive moment," constitutes a *series of decisions* that ultimately converge in one representation.

Beyond the simple formal alteration of images, this question has to do with the dialectic process that Meyer uses to articulate his pictures, making their elements function as a counterpoint not only to the interior of a photograph itself, but also when he groups a series of photographs in order to establish a more complex discourse. The critic Raquel Tibol commented on this characteristic: "The subjects saturate the entire surface of the photograph, they do not exist as a nucleus between neutral spaces because the first levels have been involved as much as the last levels," in such a manner that, "This style, eloquent in itself, seems to express itself fully when it is applied to a confrontation between two modes of individual and social behavior."[10]

By applying these principles to his recent images, Meyer has redefined one of the decisive forms of art in the 20th century: the montage. Working in montage has caused Meyer's photographs to be considered in relation to film. His digital work, however, inverts the notion of film as "images in motion" by redefining photography as "fixed film," a process, like memory, that distills a multitude of visual images into one single paradigmatic image.

The attachment to the moment that photography had before digitization has now taken a relative role, opening the possibility of examining it according to ideas such as those expressed in his time by Russian filmmaker Sergei Eisenstein, who—just like Meyer today—did not conceive of montage merely as a formal resource, but rather as a creative detonator that allowed the artist to link his work directly to perception, that is to

10. Raquel Tibol, "Pedro Meyer," in *Photographic Episodes*. Mexico, Proceso, 1989, p. 283.

The Meyers, 1940/2000.

Natasha Gelman, 1987.

say, "to the primary phenomenon of the human mind's capacity for creating images." Given that, if the basis of the cinematographic aesthetic implies "the creation of movement from the collision of two immobile forms," thanks to montage, "in the strict sense, what is produced in this case is not movement; instead our consciousness reveals its capacity for joining two separate phenomena in one generalized image, to fuse two immobile phases in one image of movement."[11]

Paraphrasing Eisenstein, in the case of digital photography the possibility of uniting two or more images in a third implies a reconsideration of the medium's reproductive capacity, not under the conditions of an analogy but with the potential of the "generalized image" described by the filmmaker, which fully takes on the possibilities of metaphor, and therefore, of the work as a form of knowledge.

Digitization, Critique, and Reality

In his great, critically insightful book *The Cult of Information*,[12] Theodore Roszak refers to the premonition that Descartes had when he dreamed of the Angel of Truth, who through "a blinding revelation, as fleeting as lightning, showed him a secret with which he would lay the foundations of a new way of thinking and of a new and wonderful science." After that dream, Descartes never again evoked the Angel of Truth. As Roszak states, in Descartes's later writings there was no "place for the role of dreams, revelations, intimate insights

11. Theodore Roszak, *The Cult of Information*. Mexico, Conaculta, 1994.
12. S. M. Eisenstein, *Toward a Theory of the Montage*. Barcelona, Paidos, 2001, p. 150.

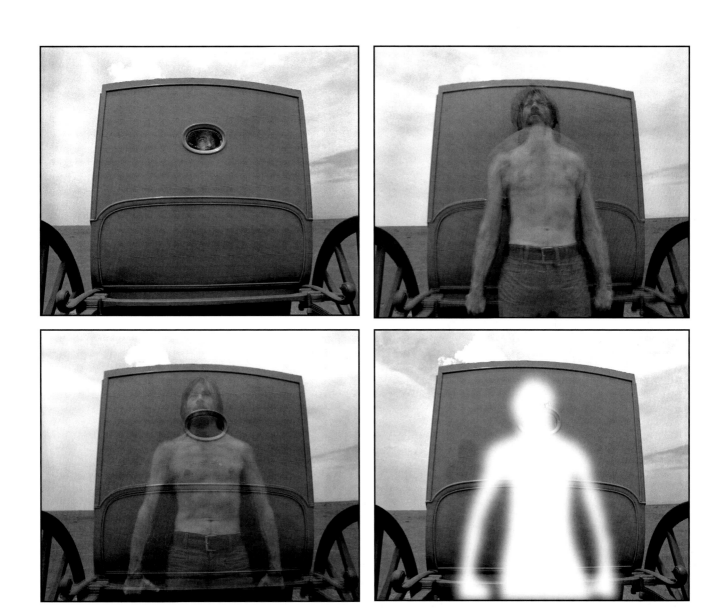

The Evil and Its Visitations,1975/1976.

as wellsprings of thought. Instead, he dedicated all his attention to logical, formal, procedures, which supposedly started with nothing, from a position of radical doubt." From then on the mysterious origin of ideas remained hidden by the powers of science and technology, the results rather than the principles of one of our most precious values: creativity.

One of the symbolic images of Pedro Meyer's work, *The Annunciation*, allows us to see how the creative dimension, beyond the media, resides in the will to face up to the photographic act just as Roszak alludes to the experience of knowledge, possible when one has "a mind that is open and receptive on all sides" in a manner such that "the strange, the peripheral, the hazy and fleeting" remain trapped in an image: possible invocation of the Angel of Truth, an ethereal figure, in the same way that the image of the boy that appears in the photograph represents a yearning before an uncertainty. A consciousness of the value of the new and of the surprising before an affirmation of permanence.

Meyer's work responds this way to the Jewish origin of his cultural identity, Roszak writes: "For the ancients the future was always a repetition of the past.... For the Jews, history was full of moral lessons. But the moral does not suppose that history repeats itself, rather it implies something new; a process unfolding through time, whose direction and end we cannot know... It is what Nahum Sarna called 'the universal duty of continuous self-learning... the connections between liberty and creativity that are found just beneath life's surface.'"

Nevertheless, Meyer's propositions cannot be attributed to just one wellspring of thought and experience: On different occasions he has renewed the role of Latin American and Mexican culture as the starting point that allows him to move with certainty between counterposed realities, articulating them from a mestizo perspective and with a vision that connects him, on the one hand, with the world of magic and ritual of one part of Mexican culture, and, on the other, with the Central European anarchism espoused by many members of the Jewish community who emigrated to America fleeing the fascism of the period between the world wars and who regularly visited his father's house during his formative years.

In analyzing Meyer's work in the photographer's 1995 book, *Truths and Fictions*, Joan Fontcuberta has pointed out the divergence between the digital images, which correspond to a speculative rather than a linear dimension, that originated in the instinct to process information, that is, to say, to speak, to store, order, and evaluate data to generate understanding—as opposed to the principles that govern analog photography, the culmination of "the instinct to imitate [and], the obsession with representing nature."[13] In the division provoked by this difference, one finds the starting point Meyer uses to recognize, paradoxically, the convergence of two needs also cited by

---

13. Joan Fontcuberta, "Pedro Meyer: Truths, Fictions and Reasonable Doubts," in Pedro Meyer, *Truths and Fictions*. "The photograph's journey from documentary to digital." Mexico, Aperture-Casa de las Imgenes, 1995, p. 10.

Fontcuberta: the mystical (religion and art) and the practical (economics, politics, business).

For someone like Pedro Meyer, accustomed to taking his place in the margins of the different cultures that run through his identity, the digital era has been a propitious space for modulating and qualifying the meaning the images acquire and the concepts that underlie them, especially at a time in which technological advances reinforce the habitual relation of photography to Western mass culture, which emphasizes understanding reality as fiction. By pointing to the social contradictions resulting from this understanding, Meyer reintroduces photography's greatest legacy: its critical potential, avoided by the tradition that made it an auto-da-fe rather than a means to knowledge.

For this reason, by integrating photography, culture, and technology in one analytical model, Pedro Meyer's work reminds us that we are witnesses to a historical change in our perception and invites us to consider the advisability of adopting heresy as a system of understanding. In other words, a permanent doubt and questioning of our ideas about what we observe is, without a doubt, the only way for us to truly penetrate the mysteries to which the images of the 20th century give rise.

Alejandro Castellanos is the director of the Centro de la Imagen, Mexico's largest center for the photographic arts.

Healer, South Africa, 2002.

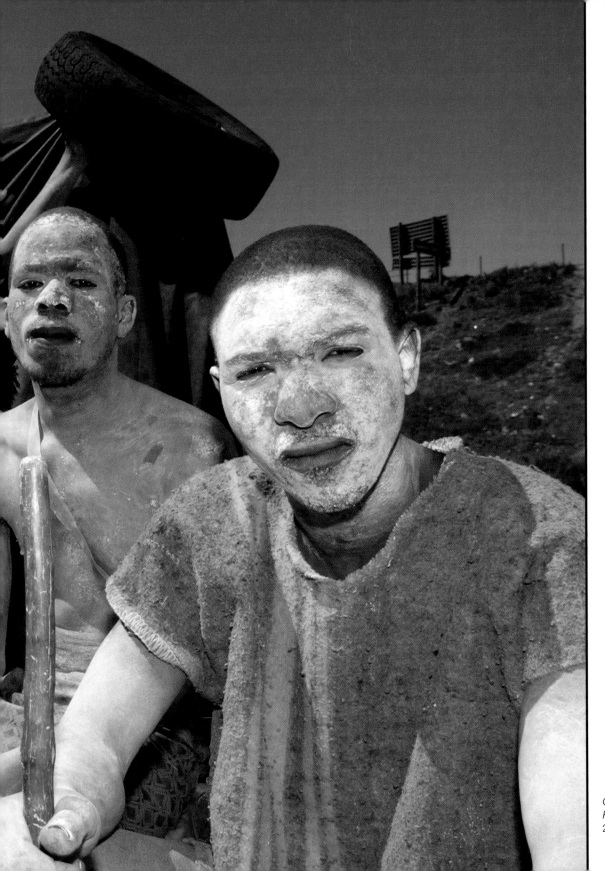

Circumcision Initiation Rites, South Africa, 2002.

María, South Africa, 2002.

José, South Africa, 2002.

Mrs. Mbeki, mother of the South African
president, South Africa, 2002.

Goodwin Makongolo, editor of *Ilizwe*, a newspaper aimed
at black readers in the Eastern Cape, South Africa, 2002.
The picture was taken on the road between the city of
Port Elizabeth and the Eastern Cape town of Grahams-
town, famous for its university.

Dr. Mangconde Mali, faith healer and "philanthropist"
from the village of Zigodlo in the heart of Ciskei, one of
South Africa's former homelands, 2002.

East London, South Africa, 2002.

In the Village of Zigodlo in the Heart of Ciskei, one of South Africa's
former homelands, 2002.

Rural Life, Waiting for the Bus in the Transkei, South Africa, 2002.

ZoneZero Editorials

By Pedro Meyer

Are Scars Beautiful?

[August 1998, www.zonezero.com]

ARE SCARS BEAUTIFUL? That depends on the beholder, doesn't it? Scars invoke the memory of difficult moments. One could argue that society tries to avoid scars. In the first world many women and men try to keep the scars of time away through the use of cosmetics and surgery, suggesting that they—the wrinkles—reveal age and ought to be something we erase. However, men are more willing to offer their scars as proof of having survived under duress; it's debatable that it exemplifies their maleness.

How our likeness appears within a picture is at times a difficult discussion. We all want to put the best spin on what we perceive to be the best angle. I believe this is a very legitimate attitude, but it is not always well understood. That is because sometimes the subject is mistaken as to what makes him or her look good. Again, there is no universal correct response to such an issue, either. No one can assure that presenting one's scars, or wrinkles, is going to lead to anyone's approval; the ultimate measure is how the subject feels about it all, regardless of the end result.

The struggle seems to be between the photographer's creative impulses and the person depicted in the image. In more advanced societies the rights of the person photographed are protected through the use of model release forms, which insure that the person in the image is comfortable with the photograph and consents to its publication.

But what happens to those who are less protected by a legal system, where there is no recourse? Photographers have traditionally traveled throughout the world considering it their God-given right to imprint their film with anyone's image regardless of what his or her opinions about the subject might be. I myself have participated extensively in this double standard of asking permission when the circumstance demanded that I do, and neglecting to do the same with those who were less understanding about the photographic process. I am not proud of my lopsided approach, but the truth is that this is what has happened and most probably will continue in the future, as much as I'd like to avoid it.

At stake in this debate is our freedom as photographers vs. the individual rights of those depicted in our photographs. I refer to freedom as in creative expression or documentary responsibility. There are no easy answers. Imagine a photographer documenting the atrocities perpetrated in a war zone—asking for permission to make pictures would be the last thing on his or her mind. Or what about photographing someone walking on the street? Is that a space that belongs to the public domain, and therefore asking to make pictures does not make sense? Or are there exceptions to such situations?

For photographers, the argument has been that "if I asked" the photographic moment (decisive moment?) would have been lost by the time I could have received permission. But in all fairness this argument is not as solid as it sounds, because there is no difference between the "photographic moment," which could have been lost, when it happens in the first world and one that happens in a third world situation. If photography can still be carried out within the framework where strict approval is required in the first world, then one also has to make the effort in situations—such as war or circumstances in the so-called third world, where people are less experienced with being photographed by a stranger—that might be more relaxed about such questions. It's about justice, isn't it?

To take a shortcut is very tempting for a photographer. Why ask for permission when it is not strictly required? And the answer is rather simple: Because, when possible, the courtesy of "asking rather than grabbing" is seen all over the world as the preferable choice. The question then becomes, do we need or want to be courteous all the time?

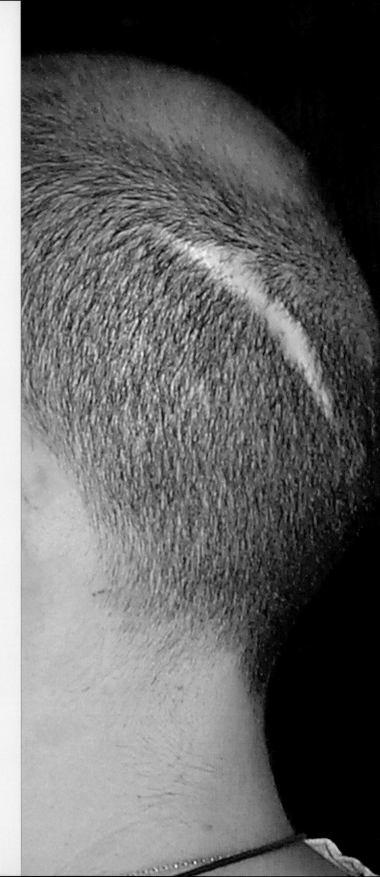

Fragment of Manuel Rocha, 1998.

In a perfect world the response is obvious. That leaves the other half of the question unanswered: What about in an imperfect world, what should it be? I know, "grabbing" is unavoidable in an imperfect world. For instance, in photojournalism, a scenario could be that while I would ask for permission, my competing colleague already grabbed the image. Solution? As in all such cases, there are no fast and easy answers. To establish rules that are universal would be sheer folly because the image-making process is too complex for one-dimensional rules.

So, let us get back to requesting permission to publish, which is not always possible—sometimes you can't locate the people in an image. Also there are situations where the simple participation of the person or persons in a picture is tantamount to an informal model release. This occurs as when a friend allows another to make a picture of her or him, or a relative willingly participates in the ritual of picture taking. One also has to recognize that many of the issues around a model release have less to do with satisfying the subject's control over his or her image than with the economic issues of making money from the sale of a picture.

Most recently, with the advances of digital technology, I have been able to show those I photograph the results right away. My camera has a small monitor to show the picture as soon as the shutter is pressed. I show the picture, and my subjects either like it or don't, and we continue with our visual explorations. The subjects are hesitant when looking at themselves, no one seems to like how they look (and neither does anyone like how their voice sounds), and very often they are not quite sure how they really feel about the image.

My reassurance becomes very important during those moments of anxiety when a gaze is exchanged, suggesting the subject's question: " I don't look good in that picture, do I?"

Yes, you look great! Remember, scars are the evidence of life. There are other scars, however, that are not external, and for the thoughtful photographer these can be seized as well. The challenge is to enter those spaces mostly with permission.

Las Vegas: Where Does Reality Reside?

[December 1998, www.zonezero.com]

W**HY AM I SO FASCINATED** by Las Vegas? Probably because it is the only place where I can make a photograph that looks like a textbook rendition of a layered digital fabrication created on a computer. A picture that is, to use a term very much appreciated by documentary photographers, a strictly "straight image." However, this photograph is a deception in that it appears to be a composite of several images. It looks "fake." But what do you call an image in which the subject matter's appearance is fake to begin with? This question takes us back to those basic dilemmas about photography: Where does the deception lie, in the original subject or in the reproduction? Or, in fact, does the deception reside in our interpretation of it all?

Twenty-five years ago, Robert Venturi, a then little-known Yale professor, arrived in Las Vegas with two dozen of his students and stayed at the Stardust Hotel. The result of that trip would become his influential 1972 book, *Learning from Las Vegas*, written with coauthors Denise Scott Brown and Steven Izenour, which introduced the

Leaving Las Vegas, Las Vegas, 1998.

Las Vegas II, Las Vegas, 1998.

Las Vegas III, Las Vegas, 1998.

Opposite: *Las Vegas I*, Las Vegas, 1998.

Las Vegas IV, Las Vegas, 1998.

world of high culture to the notion of what later became known as Post-Modernist architecture.

Today every big-city downtown has new sky-scrapers that attempt to look like old skyscrap-ers. Almost every suburb has a shopping center decorated with phony arches, fake pediments, and imitation columns. Venturi's manifesto stat-ing that Las Vegas could become a beacon for the architecture of the future, in particular in the United States, transformed such esthetic thinking throughout the world. We now see such buildings from Mexico City to London, and in major cities across the U.S. landscape.

A full-size reproduction of the Piazza di San Marco in Venice, Italy, with all the surrounding world-famous architectural landmarks, is now being built in Las Vegas. Consider the famous Campanile tower: While it's a handsome con-struction, and the subject of high praise by many critics, including John Ruskin in his exalted book *The Stones of Venice*, the one now standing in Venice isn't even the real tower. The original one collapsed in 1902 and a new tower was built in 1912—a reproduction, not the authentic article. You get the picture?

As we enter the digital age, Las Vegas will not only extend its influence the way it did for archi-tecture, but our notions of what passes as "reality" itself will also increasingly become the subject of many agonizing thoughts.

Today, at the entrance to the Warner Bros. stu-dio store in Las Vegas, Bugs Bunny, riding in a Roman chariot, presides over a collective of car-toon characters all dressed as Romans. As the fa-mous bunny stands in his vehicle, off to the left in a niche, dressed like any Roman of substance,

is the Road Runner character, presenting us with his shield as any good soldier standing in a niche would do. Such a store is for children, I assume, yet it's located amidst hundreds of slot machines that lead casino visitors to the store entrance.

At the opposite end of the Forum Shops at Cae-sars Palace is a sort of baroque moon colony, completely sealed off from the outside world, with computer-controlled sky effects that cycle from rosy-fingered dawn to purple dusk on the roof vaults above. There's also a pastiche of Roman statuary—Mickey Mouse and Donald Duck look-ing their best in Roman attire. They are feast-ing under an inscription that reads "The Ides of March." The feast is reminiscent of a Last Supper. Now why would Mickey and Donald celebrate with such relish just when Julius Caesar was about to be murdered, as the painting suggests? Can this be the decoration for a children's store?

Is Las Vegas for children? Yes and maybe. In spite of the numerous families that arrive with their kids, I hardly consider Las Vegas child oriented. At the very most it is tolerant of children, but only to a degree. Consider the sign at the entrance to the

Las Vegas V, Las Vegas, 1998.

would want to lose those exquisite palm trees (made out of plastic) that line a promenade for all the guests of the casino? The fact that the palm trees are all identically bent out of shape does not seem to be of any major concern to anyone. The precious bougainvilleas are also fake, like the huge stones from which tons of water cascade into a river. Even the butterflies are mechanical or electronic reproductions set to flap their colorful wings without interruption, day in and day out. Obviously, not all of the Mirage's rain forest is artificial; it's a careful blend of the real with the unreal: real water with plastic stones, real plants with fake butterflies, real tourists with surrogate ones (security people).

Just as Las Vegas has been a forerunner for postmodernist architecture, I believe that this incredible city, which operates at full steam 24 hours a day, can in time become the cultural capital of the world. We already have Van Gogh, Monet, Cezanne, and Picasso making their first appearances there, and cities like Paris, Venice, New York, Cairo, and Rome are well on their way to being re-created; the list is sure to grow.

I cannot wait for someone in the 21st century to make a city attempting to imitate Las Vegas—in Japan, for instance. Just imagine: The builders of such a city would have to reproduce a large chunk of the world already reproduced in Las Vegas; a copy of the copy, now that is an idea. While all of this happens Las Vegas will remain a photographers' paradise, as well as a cultural frontier, a place to explore the intellectual intricacies of where reality resides. Jorge Luis Borges had it right in *The Aleph* when he described the magical point where all places are seen from every angle.

All images were taken with a Kodak Digital Science 260 camera.

Treasure Island or Mirage casinos: "Only guests of the hotel can bring in their children sitting in strollers." Yet the Treasure Island has a free show every two hours that attracts thousands of families with children, and the Mirage has spent many millions of dollars to house a family of dolphins and create a little zoo, allegedly for the entertainment and "education" of the younger ones.

Disney World in Orlando, Florida is about tightly scripted fun for the kids. However, as Kurt Andersen wrote in Time magazine, "Las Vegas in spite of all the theme-park entertainment remains the epicenter of the American id, focused on the darker stirrings of chance, liquor and sex. If it is now acceptable for the whole family to come along to Las Vegas, that's because the values of America have changed, not those of Las Vegas."

The Mirage casino offers us a glimpse of the ever-increasing ersatz realities that in time might become the "real" things. The lobby of the Mirage is offered to us as a tropical rain forest, never mind that this is the desert—or, better said, it is there *because* this is the desert. From this "rain forest," we are told by the promotional videos on the tram leading to the casino, we should learn the importance that a rain forest holds for human life. Who

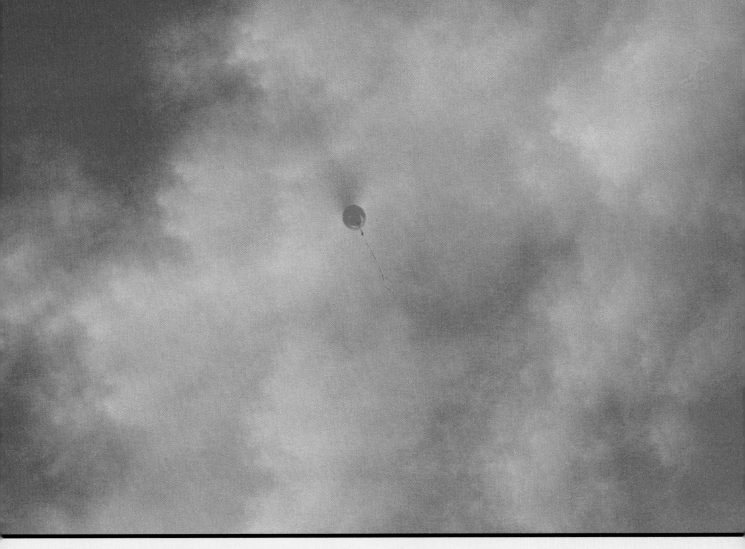

Las Vegas VI, Las Vegas, 1998.

Las Vegas VII, Las Vegas, 1998.

Las Vegas VIII, Las Vegas, 1998.

There's No Way Like the American Way

[December 1999, www.zonezero.com]

I **WAS RECENTLY DRIVING** down one of the beautiful avenues of Washington, D.C., with a friend when all of a sudden my eye caught a billboard above that archetype of Americana, a diner. The interesting thing was that the billboard I was looking at was a bit of Americana itself, a sign made famous in the 1937 photograph by Margaret Bourke-White, created at the time of the Louisville flood.

The billboard I am making reference to is "There is no way like the American Way." When I first saw it, all sorts of bells started to chime in my head about issues related to digital photography, in addition to all the social and political implications of the image itself.

I was struck by how fast we read meanings into an image, meanings that are beyond the information conveyed by the picture. In the case of Bourke-White's Louisville flood image, we see a queue of black people standing in line. We do not know exactly what they are waiting for. Given the floods, they could be waiting for transportation, or for food, or to see a doctor. Because they are standing in line, and because they are black, we view them

as being poor. What emerges is an immediate association of those who are privileged (the white people in the car in the billboard) and the "poor" (the black people standing in line). But look at the picture again and you'll see that most of the folks in the line are very well attired and do not appear to be poor. They could, for all I know, be professionals and middle class—if not all, then at least some of them. I could even imagine some of the men in the line trading places with the white man behind the wheel of the car on the billboard. One does not need digital manipulation to alter the meaning of a picture; we do a pretty good job ourselves with *straight* pictures.

What impressed me on that Washington drive was that I knew the billboard above the diner from a photograph, and I immediately associated it with the Bourke-White image. I concluded right away that the present-day billboard had to be a rip-off from her photo, even though I had no evidence to support my speculation. Upon further introspection, I reconsidered my judgment. First of all, the original billboard, the one in the Bourke-White picture, and which, in my eyes, *makes* her picture, was like so much in our history of photography—

©Margaret Bourke-White.

Diner, 1999.

an image that belonged intellectually and artistically to someone other than the photographer. Bourke-White used that billboard in a very articulate manner, to make her *successful* picture, even though it did not *belong* artistically to her.

It is only today, with so much debate about who has the copyright to what, and in particular under the jurisdiction of any alleged "digital rip-off," that such legal matters start to come to our attention. As a photographer if you today include in your picture frame a large portion of an image of intellectual property belonging to someone else, as Bourke-White did in hers, there would be all sorts of raised eyebrows, to say the least.

The original billboard is so much a part of the Bourke-White picture that I had unwittingly handed over to her the intellectual property rights for that billboard. So much so, that when I saw it independently from her picture, I assumed right away that it had been "lifted" from her photograph. For all I know that might have been the case, but even if it was so, that billboard still did not belong to her. So did she have a right to use it? Yes, in 1937; in 1999, I'm not so sure. That is something that concerns me greatly.

As a working photographer, I wish that we could have the same freedom today as Bourke-White did in 1937, but at the same time we have to contend with all sorts of additional issues of contemporary life related to photography (digital or not), which have not been sufficiently addressed. One could argue that the moment a sign is located on the street it becomes public domain. But is this really the case? I don't think so, as I imagine advertising companies are very careful to defend such an issue so their creative efforts are not vulnerable to imitation.

In Mexico, for instance, the government intervenes just as nefariously as do the private sector corporations in the United States, with their efforts to privatize everything visual. I dare say the Mexican government even took the model from the latter. To give you an example, the huge cultural heritage of all Mexico's archeological sites, instead of belonging to the people, as it ought to, is off limits to anyone wanting to photograph any of those places or artifacts found in them. The argument that the government uses to impede photography is that they are "protecting" whatever it is that they think they are guarding. However, as soon as you pay whatever sum they deem appropriate, those concerns vanish promptly.

Imagine the French trying to regulate the imagery of the Eiffel Tower, or the United States restricting photography of the Statue of Liberty. However, that is what has happened in Mexico. You have to have a permit to photograph at any archeological site, and if you want to use your images for commercial use, you have to pay a hefty royalty fee. There is a certain logic behind trying to raise funds when the use is going to be commercial, but the argument is a very slippery one—who has the rights to such intellectual property when you are dealing with public patrimony? This is not something that is discussed and regulated in an open forum with public disclosure.

So, when and how does a *public space* become public in the physical world? When does something become *public domain*? Where on the Internet is there a public space, if any? Given the digital tools that we have today, one could well take any picture and place it within a *street image* as if it were a billboard and then show it publicly over the Internet. Would that turn it into a *public domain* image?

"I Want To Marry the Sky"

[January 2000, www.zonezero.com]

IN 2000, THE ZAPATISTA MOVEMENT in Chiapas invented a place in the Southern Mexico jungle that went by the name of La Realidad (reality). It became a geographic rallying point from which to launch many of the Zapatistas' political communiqués. Although La Realidad hardly existed, the fact is that it became a reality through repetition and the clever use of all media. The Internet helped to bring much of the world's attention to what transpired in those parts of the globe no one was paying attention to.

Around the same time, faced by the onslaught of digital barbarians who were willing to engage in what was considered a despicable practice—manipulating images of reality in their computers—photographers, editors, and not a few critics, started to rally around the notion that the "reality of the image," and thus photography, had to be saved from any digital assault. The representation of "Reality" (with a capital R) had to be defended at all costs.

Documentary photographers were often at the center of those arguing against all forms of digital representation. In some quarters it was considered the root of all evil, which eventually would erode the credibility of the photographic image.

Symposia and panel discussions were organized with photographers, editors, and publishers from

Next..., 2000.

TIMES SQUARE
NEW YORK

2000 LIVE

New Millennium,
2000.

major publications, who would try to shame each other into acceptance as to what constituted an acceptable practice and what did not. (It is fascinating to observe how fast all the trappings of an inquisitorial practice can be erected.) It was determined, for instance, that images had to be labeled clearly to separate those that had suffered an alteration from those that were "pure," i.e. not modified (whatever that meant).

In order to avoid manipulation of the photographic image, codes of "ethics" were drawn up using arguments that themselves were based on words and ideas manipulated in very questionable ways. The central distortion was that all other media (written word, audio, video) were apparently considered less prone to the dangers of manipulation than those posed by photography. To extract a few minutes from an hour of audiotape or from a video interview was seen by journalists as a legitimate activity. However, if a photographer took an equivalent action—for instance, by deleting a pack of cigarettes or a telephone pole from a picture—he or she had committed major sin. Never mind that by framing a picture differently at the time of making it, one could obviate the unfortunate telephone pole without being taken to task for manipulating the representation of reality. After all, a photograph has always been a proof of reality, has it not? Now it turns out *The New York Times*, in a very interesting article, "On CBS News, Some of What You See Isn't There," by Alex Kuczynski, published on January 12, has just denounced CBS and its news program for inserting the CBS logo on top of the NBC one that appears in real life in Times Square. CBS did so during a live transmission at the time of the New Year celebrations in New York. The fact is that the genie of altering reality has been brought out of the bottle and I believe nothing can put it back in.

To tamper with a photograph, something that is understood in most cultures as "proof of reality," is such a profound issue that it has been placed in the context of a major moral problem. Some have gone so far as suggesting that digital images no longer qualify as photographs. A digital photographer would therefore be expelled from the society of his or her peers and declared a non-photographer. We have been told: "Thou shalt not alter a photograph," and if you do, you have to place corresponding warning labels all over the neighborhood, announcing your transgression. (The *Times* article states that a CBS official said that Dan Rather "knew about the use of the virtual technology during the broadcast and did not protest the practice.")

The double standard doesn't seem to bother anyone. You can manipulate anything you want, without it becoming a cardinal sin, as long as you do so before the legendary click. No problem in using makeup to embellish the color and tone of the skin, but if you dare to correct something once the picture has been shot you must acknowledge that "reality" has been tampered with.

Yes, you can use any filter you like, as long as they are optical ones and in front of the lens, but be aware that once the picture has been taken this same effort is called manipulation. Feel free to use the film of your choice to enhance the visual interpretation of the image, but consider yourself damned if you similarly enhance your picture post click, using the computer.

The problem with the accusations by *The New York Times*, or the Dan Rather mea culpa, or the excuses presented by CBS, is that while they make all this fuss about the logo being there or not, nothing is ever discussed about how real news is manipulated behind the scenes at these institutions. It is a charade to take issue with the substitution of one corporate news logo for another when there has been ample evidence that those organizations have been complicit in altering facts in the interest of political or financial expediency. Suppressing certain news is as much about manipulation of reality as blocking out one corporate logo with another.

Double Dating

Since I produced one of the earliest bodies of digital work, and I did not care to have an inquisition pass judgment on my integrity, I devised a solution that offered two dates for those images that I'd altered in the computer. One date indicated the day when the basic image was taken (on film, at the time); the second date indicated when the image was altered in the computer. Thus, you could quickly tell if something had been altered by observing if I offered two dates or one. People would actually go around my exhibitions trying to guess if something had been done to the picture or not, and then look at the dates.

Twenty-five years ago, I made the following image with the man resting under his three hats. The obvious distortion of the column shooting off towards the left was the by-product of using a wide-angle lens on a 35mm camera. I have always had a preference for wide-angle lenses; they somehow bring you in closer, but they also distort reality. Do they ever! (Can you imagine if the world really looked the way it does through wide-angle lenses, with all the unstable buildings and their parts always at odd angles?)

Now that I work with the computer, I've taken another look at that image, and fixed the distorted column. Today, the question (for all those who shout foul at the very thought of using the computer to alter photographs) is which "reality" is a more accurate representation of that which was—the one where the column is at an angle, or the one where it is now straight? Never mind that the picture is in black and white, which oddly enough is not a problem for photography purists, as if the world were actually devoid of colors.

Again, as in earlier examples, if the adjustment had been done "in camera" with a bellows on a 4 × 5, all would be acceptable; if done with the aid of the computer after the fact, everyone seems to be up in arms. I am sure you get the point about how we need to move forward and forget all this nonsense about the manipulation of digital photographs. Face it, all photographs are and always have been the product of manipulating reality. They are simply interpretations by the photographers who made them.

As we are faced by a new millennium, to those who question the term *photography* when applied to digital imagery, let me just remind you that

The Corner of Three Hats, Lazaro Cardenas, 1980.

The Corner of Three Hats, Lazaro Cardenas, 1980/2000.

photography means *writing with light*. It does not demand that such writing with light be accomplished through chemical means or electronic ones; we are fortunately left to pursue our own choices. As I see it, irrespective of which process we use, they are all photographs as long as they include the magic word: *light*.

The beauty of light as the sun sets was best described by my 4-year-old son, Julio. The other afternoon as we visited a friend, he was so enthralled by the colors in the sky that he declared to his mother and me, "I want to marry the sky."

I suspect that if we responded to reality with a mind as open as my son's, and allowed the emotion of light to become part of our awareness, we would appreciate the irrelevance of the present debate, as long as the image conveyed the message we wanted.

Obviously every one of you viewing this image will see somewhat different colors as no two monitors are identical. So which one is the true representation of the reality of that moment? What colors was Julito looking at that afternoon in Los Angeles, California, as the millennium rolled around and I recorded the moment with a camera without film?

As we start the new century we need to have a reality adjustment with regard to all these topics.

Jonathan's Street, 2000.

Redefining Documentary Photography

[April 2000, www.zonezero.com]

WHEN PRESENTING SOME of my digital pictures, I am frequently confronted with the comment: "But surely this is not a documentary photograph, is it?"

Before I respond, let's first establish what we understand a documentary photograph to be. As I see it, the intentions of a documentary photographer are to record some aspects of reality by producing a depiction of what the photographer saw, which purports to represent that reality in as objective a manner as possible.

If we can agree with that description, I can already see our critics pounding on their desks (with some degree of glee on their faces) as they suggest that this is precisely the reason there is no room for the computer to be used in re-creating documentary images.

I believe we have already discussed in many forums the fact that photography per se is tantamount to manipulation—that the impact of the lens selected, the film chosen, and all the other technical variables leave ample room to question the so called "faithful representation" of reality. So let us not mull over this one endlessly; I think it thins the debate rather than enhances it.

Today, let's explore the parallels between photography and other forms of documentary work. For instance, a journalist brings together his writings, which represent a synthesis of what he saw and/or heard, by what he imagines are the lines of reason behind the information selected. The journalist is not a copy machine that mindlessly reproduces what is placed on the platen. Employing his own decision-making process, the journalist weaves together information in a way that he believes will present an accurate story.

A documentary filmmaker does not shoot film or video without an editing process in mind. We only assume that the people in the documentary are not hired, that they are real-life characters, and that the settings are also real environments rather than constructed sets. Of course one can go on from profession to profession related to documentary work, and you will always find the same sort of rationale: a belief that the representation

¿Donde Esta la Lana? (Where is the Money?), Ecuador, 1985/2000.

was based on real-life situations and that the information, however real, still had to be processed and edited before it was presented to the public.

So why are so many people up in arms about the idea that a computer-edited photograph is not a true documentary representation? As I understand, it has mainly to do with past traditions and customs. It apparently flies in the face of reason that even though an image has been altered, it can still call itself a document. What is wrong in

that analysis is that any and all alterations have been treated equally (they are all bad). We know for a fact that not all alterations have the same justifications behind them, that some alterations can even enhance the veracity of an image. Furthermore, many of the fears related to the conceptual changes in photography have mainly to do with a loss of certainty of what the photograph actually is delivering—as a document—with little debate about the veracity of the content of a given image.

We are dealing here with the same ethical debates around editing a story, whether employing text, audio, or film, that people have been engaging in for a long time. For photography it is no different. Why should it be? If anything is different it's because in the past we could not reasonably edit photography in the way we can today, so when the tools first appeared that empowered us to do so, everyone ran for the exits. All those other mediums had always been edited and were malleable to the nth degree; photography, in that sense, was less flexible. Not that one could not alter docu-

mentary images, just ask the Soviets about all that they did in this respect. I maintain that photography has always lived a life of false pretenses. Today when we intend to remove that disguise all sorts of defense lines are drawn.

Of course photography can lead to deception; it always could. What is more, its open-ended nature insofar as meaning goes has always been used to support the intentions of the photographer. The digital age has not rushed in an avalanche of alterations, as some thought would happen. If one looks around at what is being produced and called photographs one will discover that these are mostly illustrations. Another category that has grown recently is that of expanding the realm of the "fantastic," again with no attachment to the real world. What is less evident, however, is the work that is being produced that looks like traditional photographs but is created with non-traditional, digital methods. The reason for this is obvious: Unless you are willing to reveal how you made the image, no one can really tell what was done, provided it was done well. That is what makes people so nervous and unwilling to consider a digitally produced image as a documentary photograph.

Look at the photograph at the beginning of this essay. I decided that the title for this image would be: "Where Is the Money?" In Spanish it's a double entendre that is quite nice, as the title, "¿dónde está la Lana?" is based on *lana*, meaning money as well as wool, for instance that of the sheep in the background. And the title "Where is the money?" also references Cuba Gooding Jr. repeatedly saying to Tom Cruise, "Show me the money" in *Jerry*

Ecuador, 1985.

Ecuador, 1985.

Maguire (1996). Or in looking at the image one could also recollect that other famous phrase, "Greed is good," spoken by Michael Douglas in *Wall Street* (1987). For me it was interesting to relate such "first world" movie sentences to a reality in the "third world." I guess that when it comes to some basic human attitudes we are all alike

Interesting questions arise by the juxtaposition of the man showing us the money. Why does he hold up that money? Is he asking us to pay for something? Is he doing so because he wants money for being photographed? Is he selling us some sheep meat? Does he think he needs to pay for his photograph? What is the relation of power in that encounter between the photographer and the subject and, as an extension, us the viewers? What role do the sheep represent in all of this? Are they symbolic of something other than their physical presence?

Now, evaluate the elements that compose the image. First is the issue of the origin of the parts used. In this case the two main elements are the man holding the money and the background image with the sheep being skinned. Both pertain to the same place and were taken in contiguous moments in time. They belong together, as it were, as they have their common roots of space and time in a small village in Ecuador where I took the pictures. The only thing that did not occur in the final picture is that they appeared as they do in the photo.

The background picture is turned left to right, in order to have the light fall in the same direction in both components of the final image, as well as making space for the man holding the money.

Such an alteration I consider no different than what ordinary editing does in film, or when words are accommodated for better reading within a text. However, this leads to an interesting issue within photography—luck.

Had all these elements appeared before my camera as they are in the final picture, I would not have had to do anything further. Photographers became accustomed to the notion of "having content and geometry make an appointment," as Max Kozloff once stated so eloquently, in great part through luck. One knew one was "lucky" to have everything fall into place, even though we took full credit for all the timely decision-making abilities involved. The only problem with some of these so-called talents is that more often than not the coincidence of content and geometry coming together would not have been visible under the best of circumstances. Or worse yet, one would proceed like fishermen who go about their task casting a wide net, and then seeing what comes up in the catch. Photographers using motor-drive cameras to shoot off numerous rolls of film, shooting faster than even the eye can see, then go through their catch to discover the "good ones." The euphemism for this is *editing*.

I am not questioning the validity of patience that some great photographers have exerted in order to get at exactly the image that they imagined, but even when patience was at the core of such endeavors an element of chance would inevitably crop up.

I dislike the notion that my work be determined mainly by luck. I'd rather fail on my own efforts than attribute poor results to the absence of luck. The reverse of this argument is that I like to determine what an image looks like on the basis of my intentions, not chance. Photographers today have a wonderful opportunity that enhances their options when creating an image, and it has nothing to do with luck. Now I, like others who create documentary stories, can pull all the strings that make an image stronger, by eliminating, adding, and reorganizing the pieces of information that make up the picture.

As far as the factual evidence of "what was," the traces of light give evidence of what was there. In my picture nothing appears within the frame that wasn't there, insofar as the reality of the space. Yes, the order has been altered and changed, but then what is the difference between my computer alteration and the photographer who chooses the position of his or her camera? Or what is the difference between my computer alteration and a photographer asking, sometimes nudging ever so lightly, that the subjects he's about to photograph move to a more favorable light or position?

Some years ago, Colin Jacobson wrote a letter to me about his concern that in the future digital photographers would become increasingly sloppy, because they could, after all, erase those elements that they were too lazy to deal with in the first place. I am sure that sloppy work preceded digital technology and thus the argument about such risks only tended to obscure the rich potential for making ever better images—precisely the opposite of his concern. He was worried that the tools would be misused; I was convinced of the opposite: that they would lead to creativity, not sloppiness.

I urge photographers everywhere to test the waters, to experience coming up with documentary work that is very strong by means of applying digital technology. The risks for abuse are obviously present but they have always been there, for other mediums as well; none of this ever stopped responsible creators from using all their tools. Documentary photography has been redefined; it is time to prove it.

Trust the Photographer, Not the Photograph

PEDRO MEYER in conversation with **KEN LIGHT**

By Douglas Cruickshank

> In all affairs, it's a healthy idea, now and then, to hang a question mark on things you have long taken for granted.
>
> — BERTRAND RUSSELL

ÉNÉ MAGRITTE WAS no photojournalist, but maybe photojournalists, and those who publish their work, could take a tip from the Belgian surrealist. In the late 1920s, Magritte made a painting of a tobacco pipe. He called it *The Betrayal of Images*; in cursive text beneath the picture he inscribed the words, "Ceci n'est pas une pipe"— "This is not a pipe."

Magritte was right, of course, as many have elaborated on at length. *The Betrayal of Images* is a picture not a pipe. The point Magritte made with his painting and the assertion that Pedro Meyer has been underscoring with his photography for years may be a few degrees apart, but they reside in the same intellectual territory: that conceptual landscape where perception and misperception converge, and where reality is often confused with its representation—such as a photograph.

Meyer is a documentary photographer who—while he's done acclaimed work in what might be termed conventional photojournalism—often uses a computer to manipulate his photographs. He does this, he says, to express the truth. "All my images are about documenting experiences—not fabricating them," says Meyer. "The experience in a traditional photographic representation has been limited to those elements that the lens was able to capture. To the silver halides or dyes, I now can add my own memory."

Meyer's defense of his manipulation of his own documentary photos, and his contention that those images remain documentary in nature even after they've been digitally modified, has, for more than a decade, put him at the heart of a fascinating controversy: What is the difference, if any, between the real and the true? If a photo can be manipulated to depict a lie, can it also be manipulated to depict the truth? Many say that any manipulation of a documentary photograph creates a falsehood, but Meyer contends this isn't so. A picture can be made truer, he believes. A photograph's veracity should be judged by the integrity of the person who made it. The questions Meyer provokes are particularly timely, coming at a time when many feel that traditional journalism, and its professed pursuit of the truth, is an institution that falls far short of delivering on its promise.

Perhaps no one more vehemently disagrees with Meyer on this topic than Ken Light, a prolific, widely known social documentary photographer, who also happens to be an old friend of Meyer's. "I'm a hard liner," Light says. "Pedro knows that. I believe that digital photography does have a place in the world. It definitely can pass images quickly to news organizations, but I think the whole alteration issue is like a bad virus."

Ironically, Light, a teaching fellow and curator of the Center for Photography at the Graduate School of Journalism at the University of California Berkeley, and a founder of the International Fund for Documentary Photography, was personally infected by that virus in February of 2004 in an episode that made the national and international news. "My photograph of John Kerry was stolen and altered to show Kerry with Jane Fonda," Light explains. The original photo, which Light took at a 1970 anti-war rally in Mineola, New York, was of John Kerry, seated by himself, about to give a speech. Thirty-four years later, someone, who Light identifies as "a neo conservative, a right wing person in the Midwest," illegally downloaded the image from the Corbis Web site and skillfully combined it with a 1972 photograph of Jane Fonda taken by Owen Franken at a Miami Beach rally. The resulting composite image depicts Kerry listening appreciatively to Fonda, who's reviled by many veterans, some of Kerry's staunchest supporters. The hoax was quickly revealed, but not before the phony picture had been widely distributed throughout the world via the Internet.

Actress And Anti-War Activist Jane Fonda Speaks to a crowd of Vietnam Veterans as Activist and former Vietnam Vet John Kerry (LEFT) listens and prepares to speak next concerning the war in Vietnam (AP Photo)

Top: The skillfully made hoax photo of John Kerry and Jane Fonda that was widely distributed on the Internet is a composite image created using Ken Light's 1970 picture of Kerry and Owen Franken's 1972 photo of Fonda.

Bottom: Light's original photo of John Kerry. © 1970 Ken Light.

"That was many months ago," Light says, "and I'm still getting emails from people who say, 'We know that your image was a fake. Jane Fonda was really in the picture and you actually took her out.' And people believe this. The problem is once the virus gets out into the world, people still believe the virus and they don't necessarily hear the voices of

reason that stand up and say 'Wait a minute, this is a hoax, this is not real.' Somehow the image gets separated from the truth, and that's my concern."

Meyer shares Light's concern, but he comes at the issue from a very different direction. Not surprisingly, he also sees the solution differently than Light does. It's a fascinating conundrum, and in the interest of further exploring it, I invited Light and Meyer to get together (via telephone—Light in Berkeley California, Meyer in Mexico City) to discuss their opposing views on the digital manipulation of documentary photographs. I first asked both photographers what may seem a simple question: "What is a documentary photograph?"

"The answer is in the question," Meyer answers. "It's an image that documents something."

"It's definitely an image that documents something," Light says. "I've also described it as something that's more long-term, in-depth, independently created by a photographer—generally, not on assignment for a magazine or with an editor's oversight. It's the independent voice of the image maker."

Dr. Albert Schweitzer in the Congo, 1954. Photo by W. Eugene Smith. In the darkroom, Smith composited two images to make this picture. Schweitzer and the man behind him are from one negative. The hand and saw in the foreground are from a second negative.

In addition to numerous gallery exhibitions, both Meyer and Light have published their documentary photography extensively—as books and, in Meyer's case, on the Web and on CD. Light's books include *Delta Time: Mississippi Photographs*, *Witness in Our Time: Working Lives of Documentary Photographers*, and several others. Meyer's autobiographical *I Photograph to Remember* is a highly personal work, and one of the first such presentations to be released as a CD (in 1994). It can now also be viewed, and listened to, on the ZoneZero Web site. ("I think it was the first CD-ROM with images and sound that was done anywhere," Meyer tells me. "Sure there were images within

CD encyclopedias, and other multimedia projects, but none with the images and sound presented as one" complete linear narrative.)

"You're both familiar with the *Salon* article, 'A Picture is no Longer Worth a Thousand Words,' published in April 2004, in which you were quoted. In that piece the author, Farhad Manjoo, summarized Ken's view like so: '...he worries that the truth we see in photographs will diminish in a digital age. And that people will start to ignore real pictures as phonies. When every picture is suspect all pictures are dismissible and photography's unique power to criticize will decline.' Is that accurate?"

"That sounds pretty good," Light says.

I ask Meyer if he agrees.

"I think it's quite evident that this is not the case," he says. "If you treat photographs in the same way you treat text, then the whole problem is actually resolved. You cannot have an image be a witness to itself—as testimony of its veracity. That is impossible as a premise. The alternative is to have elements which give cross-reference to a picture. For example, that happened a long time ago in the events of Bloody Sunday, which were photographed by many photographers at the same time; what was revealed in the photos then brought into question many of the statements made by the British Government regarding how they repressed the marchers." [Meyer is referring to the January 30, 1972 incident that occurred during a civil rights march in Derry, Northern Ireland in which 27 people were shot by British soldiers.]

In the same way that written journalism is, ostensibly, checked and double-checked, or cross-referenced, as Meyer puts it, he advocates subjecting documentary photography to a similar verification regimen. "With text," he says, "somebody comes out with a major statement and you double-check that it was actually said. If you have the cross-reference of something then that is what holds it up as true. It's not because somebody wrote it down that it becomes a true statement, it's because it's been cross-referenced. And the same thing can, and will, be done with photography."

But Ken Light sees other problems in establishing the truth of a photograph. "You and I agree, Pedro, that truth is very relative—where a photographer stands, what they edit out, what they see, what lens they use, all create a personal truth of the image maker. But there's always an image maker to stand up and say, 'I was there, this is what happened, this is what I saw.' However, when that truth gets separated from the physical image, and someone looks at that image and they don't know what is real and what is not real, and whether or not it's been altered digitally..." That, Light says, is a problem, a potentially big problem for documentary photography.

"We're just starting to enter this era," Light continues. "Pedro, you were one of the very early practitioners of this. But now, you know, Joe Blow, in Missouri, can do it at his home computer, can go onto ZoneZero and download one of your images and alter it and put it out to the world and say this is real. And if you don't see it, if you don't stand up, how do you alter that reality [invented by Mr. Blow]?"

Nevertheless, Light acknowledges that the sort of thing that happened to his photo of John Kerry is now inevitable and will likely be happening with

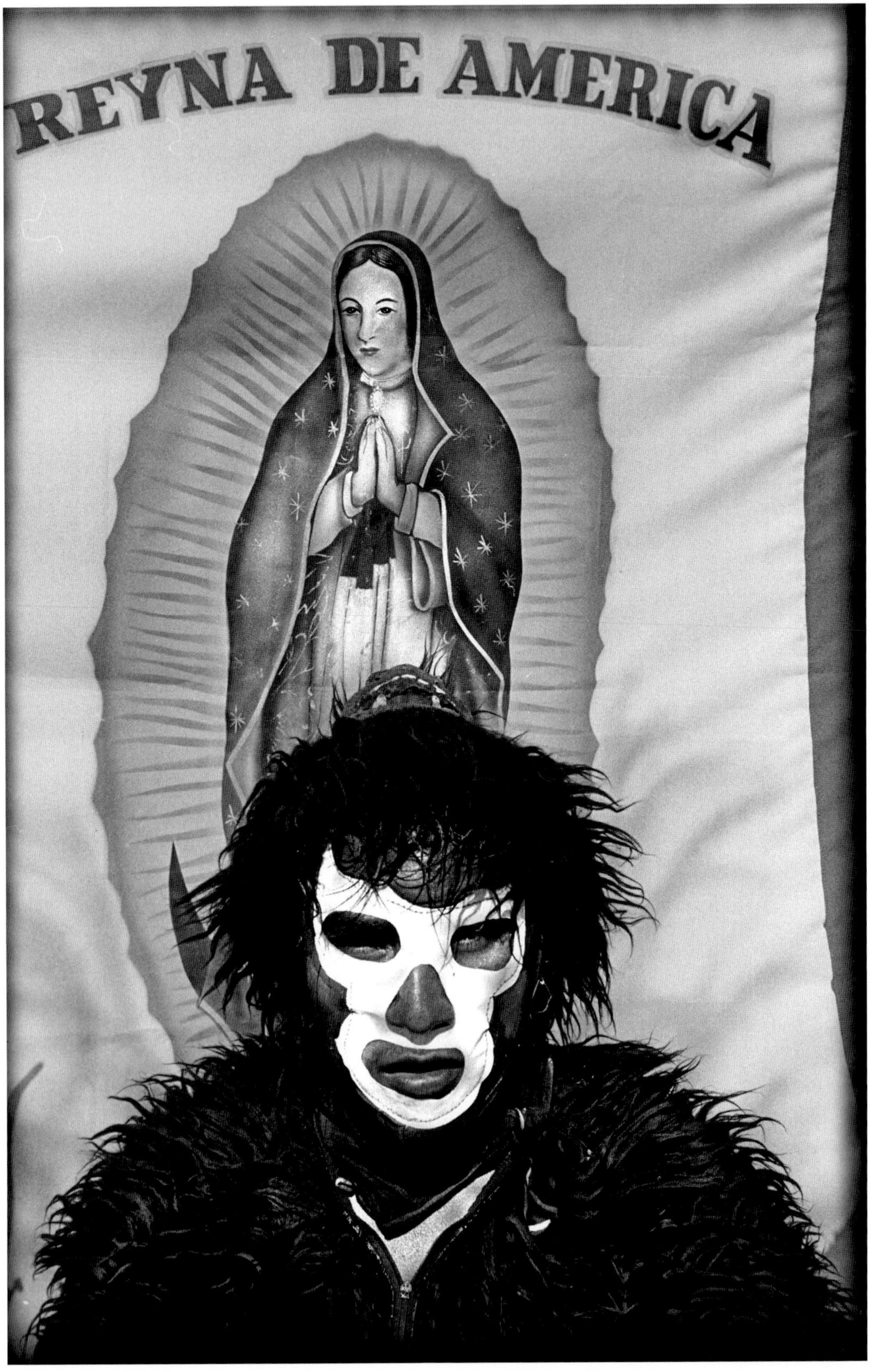
REYNA DE AMERICA

greater frequency and technical sophistication in the future—but he doesn't have to like it. Meyer, on the other hand, seems to welcome this new war on reality and those who claim to have a monopoly on recording and disseminating the truth.

"Ken," Meyer says, "what you just said is absolutely true, and I have been aware of this for a long time, but I look at the issue in reverse. You and I probably share the same goals, but where we separate is in how we get to those goals. My approach is: Let us look upon these issues in a way that takes away the wishful thinking about what would be desirable and let us then say, 'Okay, this is the way things are going to be.' Therefore, the best we can hope for is that the image no longer be the credible one; the photograph should not be credible. And the faster and the sooner everybody disbelieves the picture, the better off we are. Then Ken Light, who has a high degree of respect and who is a serious person, will be the one who has the credibility, not the picture. If you give me an image and it is signed by Ken Light, I will know that image is credible—not because it's a photograph. That's where I want this to end up."

Light listens intently to Meyer. There are a few moments of silence before he responds, "Well, I think that you're right," Light says. "We come from the opposite direction—you're on one end and I'm on the other. Ultimately we both love and respect photography. I'm not going to stop this. It's greater than me and it's marching forward. But those of us who've spent our lifetimes working in documentary photography, have, I think, a great influence—we influence the public and what the public sees and thinks about what's acceptable, and what editors will do and what they will not do. With my Kerry picture, for example, before the *New York Times* would run it, they called to

confirm whether or not it was real. The Internet did none of that. Everyone started running the picture, assuming if it was on the Internet it was real, and it appeared around the world. And, as you know, with the Internet it's like rabbits multiplying, only quicker. Photography has become more and more powerful. When we start to allow people to alter it—because it's *their* truth—that makes me nervous."

"Let's change direction," I say to Meyer, "and talk about what I see as a fundamental difference between your view of photography and Ken's view, and it doesn't have anything to do with whether it's digital or not. Ken, I think I'm correct in saying that you believe there was a time when photographs were synonymous with the truth.

"More or less," Light says.

"And, Pedro, you contend that photographs have always been illusion."

"Absolutely," Meyer says. "I think that one of the problems for Ken, and those who are like-minded, is that they have worked for a long, long time and they believe in the credibility of the image. And because they've worked with a lot of integrity, and did their work with dedication, to all of a sudden make a 180-degree turn and say, 'Okay let us assume that none of this is actually the case,' would put into question all their previous work. But that is not how I see it. If I continue with the logic that no photograph is credible simply because it's a photograph, but that it should be credible only because it was made by a credible photographer, I believe that puts Ken's work back into the picture with much more value. In other words, all of the work that he did is therefore more credible because of his life long integrity."

"I agree, Pedro, that the integrity of the photographer is very, very important. And that's something that definitely drives work," Light responds.

"The photographer's integrity is the *only* thing that's important," Meyer says.

"But who decides that, Pedro? Does it get decided in the photographer's lifetime? Does it get decided after the photographer passes on, and editors or the photography police go into their archives and they actually look. We all know that W. Eugene Smith was one of the great voices of the truth, but after he passed on people discovered that he altered photographs—before PhotoShop. He changed things."

"I don't give a damn whether he altered his pictures in the darkroom," Meyer says excitedly. "I don't give a damn whether he put two images together!"

"But you see I disagree," Light replies, "and the reason I disagree is because we make photographs for the moment, but photography also records the past. And long after we're gone, we hope, if the planet is still here, people will go back and look at those images and revisit the subjects and the individuals. And if our photographs have some truth to them, vis-à-vis the photographer, they have a new interpretation. And it opens up incredible windows and doors to the worlds that no one has ever seen before. To me that's really important."

Light continues to press his point, citing an article he read earlier in the day in the *New York Times* ("40 Years Later, Civil Rights Makes Page One," by James Dao July 13, 2004) that, he says, "completely blew me away." The *Times* story reveals how newspapers in the South choose not to report on the Civil Rights Movement, assigning neither print nor photo journalists to cover what amounted to a social revolution sweeping through the region and, indeed, the entire country. "All of sudden, "Light explains, "the editors of this newspaper have gone back, 40 years later, to ask, 'What did we do?' And they discovered all these photographs that were made in these communities by an amateur, believe it or not, who was there. And the people in the communities are shocked that they didn't know about it, and the people who were involved in the Civil Rights Movement, who were not seen struggling at the time, now, 40 years later, feel like they've had their day in court. They feel somehow seen. Photography has played an important part. So, to me, what we do now has great import, and impact, for the future."

"Sorry, Ken, you've put yourself in a very vulnerable position," Pedro says.

"Okay," Light responds with a laugh. "Checkmate."

"You've put yourself in a vulnerable position," Meyer tells Light, "because if you question the pictures of Eugene Smith because they were altered in his darkroom and you bring up all these issues of representation, well…"

"I'm just raising them as issues that are out there," Lights shoots back. "I think his photographs are very important and what he did was very important. You and I know photographers do direct in the field. They use filters. They change lenses. And they have emotion. My god, Pedro, you know, I have incredible emotion when I go out into the field and photograph—and I photograph certain things, while other things I see I choose not to photograph."

River Baptism, Moon Lake, Coahoma County, Mississippi, 1989. From Ken Light's *Delta Time* (Smithsonian Institution Press, 1995.) © 1999 Ken Light.

"Hold on," Meyer says. "Your pictures are in black and white, and reality, as far as I have been able to see, is not in black and white. Your pictures are an abstraction of reality."

Light says, "Yes, that's absolutely correct."

"You've made the decision to make your pictures in black and white," Meyer continues, "and you find that to be acceptable—so be it, but don't tell me that is a representation of truth. That is an abstraction of truth. That is your personal point of view."

Light agrees, then quickly says, "But I'm not deciding that I want to add something else to a picture I took yesterday. I mean, I could have easily decided I wanted to add Jane Fonda to my John Kerry picture, and put it out to the world, and when people called me up and asked, 'Was Jane Fonda really there?' I'd say, 'Of course she was. This is my picture. This is real. This is my truth.' Then what do we do Pedro? What happens then?"

"Ken, you cannot pick and choose what alterations you will accept or not accept. When you take the color out of reality that is your choice and you have to live with that decision. But don't tell me that taking out color is okay, but if somebody takes out another element in the picture that's not okay. Because that's what makes your whole argument questionable."

"Wait," Light tells Meyer. "I think that people are, in fact, visually trained to look at black and white—because until recently newspapers and magazines were completely black and white due to technical issues, not necessarily by choice. The conversion to color is only very recent."

I jump in and ask Light if he uses a digital camera.

"I don't," he tells me. "I use digital for eBay, which is where I think it belongs. I choose to work in black and white film because I like the craft. I like to develop, and I like to print myself, which I still do."

Light turns back to his discussion with Meyer.

"They're not just taking out elements; they're putting in elements," he says to Meyer. "For example, there's a picture of yours, which I've always liked and I don't know if it's real or not. It's a photograph of farm workers in a field and there's a billboard for a casino above them. If it's real, it's an awesome documentary photograph. If it's not real, it's an awesome art piece. But I'm wondering if it should be labeled, so that people can differentiate between the real and the created. I don't have a problem with people creating something as long as they say, 'I created this.'"

"The picture is a composite; it's black and white," Meyer replies. "And it is an example of what I have been saying. It's an image that I put together as a representation of things that happened within a mile of each other. It's a statement represented in the picture, much the same way as somebody makes a statement in text. A writer makes a composite: 'I saw this and that and the other.' You read it and it's a statement about something."

"Yes," Light says, "but there's a difference between fiction and nonfiction. To me, editing a picture is not taking two different frames and putting them together and saying, 'This is what I saw.'"

"What I am presenting," Meyer tells Light, "is the future of photography, because photographers

Mexican Migratory Workers, highway in California, 1986/1990.

now have a much greater amount of creative freedom to express how we think, how we develop ideas."

"What about this photographer, [Brian Walski], at the *Los Angeles Times*," Light asks Meyer, "who was in Iraq, and decided to do the same thing that you did with your farm worker picture? He witnessed two things and he decided 'Well, it's not such a bad thing if I put them together because really both things happened, but there was a time delay.'"

"I applaud it," Meyer answers. "Nothing of what he did made the message any different. On the contrary, it made the picture better."

"But it didn't happen; it was his own fantasy," Light says.

"What he showed," Meyer insists, "was a much better picture. It didn't change one iota the information given about the event."

"It changes what people believe," Light tells Meyer. "It changes the attitude of Americans, that the media has a liberal bias. That the media is not telling the truth."

"Exactly, that's my point," Meyer says. "Now you have it."

Light: "So we live in a fantasy world."

The two unaltered pictures (above right), taken in Iraq by *Los Angeles Times* photographer Brian Walski were used to create the composite (above left) that ran on the front page of the *Times* on March 31, 2003. Walski was fired the next day. Photos at top right and bottom right courtesy of Brian Walski.

Meyer: "Makes sense."

Meyer and Light agree to disagree, though Meyer would perhaps agree with Ralph Waldo Emerson, who once remarked, "Fiction reveals truth that reality obscures."

"There's another, related topic I'd like to hear more of your opinions on," I say. "I'm interested in hearing what you think about 'pre-click manipulations,' such as the use of filters, the use of bellows to correct architectural distortion, and similar in-camera manipulations that can have a significant effect on a photograph. I'd also like you to discuss 'post-click manipulations,' such as burning and dodging, which I think many documentary photographers and traditional photojournalists have used and continue to use."

"For me," Light says, "part of the mystery of photography is being at the moment, at the place, seeing, watching very carefully, and clicking. To me, that click is the basis of image making. Not the click of the mouse, the click of the shutter. And if you can't click the shutter at the right moment, you've made a bad picture. I don't think it's OK to then click the mouse and make it into a good picture—because you haven't been there and you haven't seen that thing. You move on and you try to learn from that experience."

I ask Light about the tools and techniques he uses when shooting: "With your death row pictures, for example, or your Mississippi Delta photos, did you use a filter?"

"'Pre-click' filters and bellows can enhance a photograph," Light replies. "They make a photograph more dramatic. I'm not against drama. I've used filters. And I use a close-up lens, a macro lens, which is unusual when working with a medium format camera—there's a certain distortion to a macro; it gives you an unnatural ability to get very, very close. It shows things that—if you were standing there—you would not see in the way the camera does. But I think that's OK, because when I take the picture I'm standing there, I see it, the camera enhances it. But I don't use PhotoShop to take a cigarette from another image, from someone else, and put it in a different guy's mouth, to make my photo look more dramatic—because the cigarette wasn't there! To me, there's a middle ground with this."

Meyer listens to Light, then says, "Think about having the liberty to use any tool you want to and to ask yourself, "What, what am I trying to get at?" I'm trying to make pictures, and trying to tell a story in the best way possible, and tell it truthfully. If that is the case, what's the purpose in discussing which tools are OK to use before or after the shutter clicks? I use anything that allows me to get to that point, to tell the story, as efficiently, practically, and productively as possible."

"The bottom line," Light says, "is that the digital genie is out of the bottle. We're not going to stop it, and that's OK. I love Pedro's work. I remember the first time I saw prints of Pedro's. They were huge and the color was beautiful. I remember the boy on the pole with the fire behind it, and the chessboard with the woman on it, floating in the air. It was amazing, very powerful; the future of photography way before anyone else was doing it. But it's art, it's not documentary, and that's OK. Maybe Pedro doesn't want to say he's an artist, which he is; I'll say it. But his work is not documentary, it's not in the documentary tradition.

Opposite: *Virgil on the Greased Pole*, Nochistlan, Oaxaca, Mexico, 1991/1992.
Above: *The Case of the Missing Painting from the Altarpiece*, Yanhuitlan, Oaxaca, Mexico, 1991/1993.

Now that may change in the future as everyone becomes a documentary photographer because they have a camera cell phone, but for me, at the moment, there's fiction and nonfiction and both of those are great reads."

Even over the long distance telephone line it's easy to tell that Meyer is moved by his old friend's opinion of his work. "I appreciate what Ken says very much, and I humbly accept his opinion, but I must say that I don't have to label myself a documentary photographer, and exclude myself from making artistic images, or vice versa." Meyer invokes the novelist and journalist Gabriel Garcia-Marquez, who began his career as a journalist, later became internationally renowned for his novels—frequently described as "magical realism"—and has continued to write both fiction and nonfiction.

He then goes back to the topic of pre-and post-click manipulations, referring to a photograph he uses in conjunction with a ZoneZero editorial, to make his case (see page 117 to read this editorial). "There's a man lying down with three hats in front of a building," Meyer explains. "The picture was taken with a wide angle lens, so a column on a building in the background is slanted, because of the lens distortion. Later, when I looked at that picture, I thought to myself, 'Isn't it interesting, this is a black and white documentary picture, yet the wide angle lens distorts everything in the field of vision.' But people have been educated to the notion of black and white and also to the fact that a wide angle lens distorts. We've educated people that these things distort reality, are an abstraction of reality, so why can't we also educate people to the notion that photographs are not credible?"

Meyer explains that he used PhotoShop to straighten the column, post-click. "Therefore that picture is today a truer representation of the actual scene at the time I took the picture. So how can one dismiss the manipulations of the computer as distorting reality?"

"I'm just saying that people should know it's altered," Light interjects.

"What if Pedro had made that correction using a bellows on his camera at the time he took the picture," I ask Light. "Do people need to know that it was altered then, or is that acceptable?"

"I think that's acceptable," Light says. "And Pedro is right, I do use a wide angle lens, and I do think people are educated to know that the camera distorts certain things, visually, but they don't yet understand what a photo illustration is or what a composite is."

"Ken," Pedro says, "let's take this conversation into the future. Just as the public's been educated about the effect of a wide angle lens, don't you think the public will get educated in regard to manipulations done in the computer?"

"Since the genie is out of the bottle," Light replies, "I would hope that's the case, but the question is whether the media, which has the power to educate people, will really do that. I don't know what the end result will be."

"But it's inevitable that's going to happen," Meyer says, "because nobody set out to educate about wide angle lenses, it just happened."

"It probably is inevitable," Light agrees. "But it's sad to me, Pedro, because I think of one of the images that I talk about with my students, the O.J. Simpson mug shot covers of *Newsweek* and *Time* magazines." [Light is referring to the June 27, 1994 issues of the two news magazines. *Newsweek* ran the Simpson mug shot unaltered, but *Time* manipulated the image. The technician that did it explained that he "wanted to make it more artful, more compelling." Controversy ensued.]

"They darkened Simpson's skin," Light explains, "so he'd look sinister. They did it in PhotoShop. Obviously someone at the news magazine thought that was OK. To me that's a little bit scary, when you start darkening peoples' skin because you have a certain agenda that you want to hoist on other people. "

"But why would you be surprised about that? Today you have the same issues going on in the Bush Administration," Meyer says, referring to President Bush being photographed with what was later revealed to be a decorative, not intended for the soldiers to dine on, turkey when he visited Iraq on Thanksgiving Day, 2003.

"But you think it's OK," Light tells Meyer.

"No I don't think it's OK," Meyer insists. "I'm not making a moral judgment, but these things are happening. What's the difference between a photo of Bush with a fake turkey and the discussion we're having?"

"The difference," Light says, is that the photographers who took that picture of the fake turkey should have stood up and said, 'We're not taking

The controversial O.J. Simpson cover, *Time* magazine, June 27, 1994.

this picture because this is a fake.' But they went ahead and did it and put the picture out there. And now we've discovered it was a fake."

"I believe that you're fighting windmills when you use the term 'should have.' Let's forget about the 'should have' because this is not going to happen," Meyer says.

"It could happen," Light says to Meyer, "if photographers stood up and demanded that photography be a certain way. You said the *Los Angeles Times* photographer, who altered the Iraq photo, was OK to do what he did. What's the difference between what he did and what the Bush people do? It's the same exact thing. Everyone thinks they're right. They both have an agenda. The photographer's agenda was probably to win the Pulitzer Prize, or to be thought of as a better photographer, so he altered the photo. I'm sure he didn't have a political agenda. The other side, they have a political agenda. And they're going to use the tools."

"And the sooner the world at large can decode and decipher these manipulations," Meyer says, "the better off we are."

And right about there is where Light and Meyer's conversation ended. Even though they see these issues from entirely different perspectives, and neither swayed the other's opinions, in retrospect it seems they're both right, which is what makes this such a complex, difficult to unravel topic. Light no doubt has a good grasp of Meyer's view, he simply doesn't believe that a documentary photograph can be altered and still be fundamentally documentary, and nothing Meyer says will convince him otherwise. Meyer, on the other hand, contends that the photograph—independent of the integrity of its maker—has never been a credible means of conveying truth; he sees no reason that documentary photographs shouldn't be edited in the same way as print journalism. Furthermore, Meyer contends that the problem of the public being duped by hoaxes—such as when Light's John Kerry photo was unscrupulously altered and distributed to news organizations worldwide—can be solved by educating people about the essentially illusory character of photography; a process that he believes will happen naturally as people become more sophisticated in their understanding of digital photography and the relative ease with which it can be manipulated. Light, however, insists that altered photos should be labeled as such, and that something of essential importance is damaged when the traditional tenets of documentary photography are no longer adhered to.

Réné Magritte, it's safe to say, would be both fascinated and amused.

At the Ganges, India, 2005.

Replicants, India, 2005.

Opposite: *Two Stories Tall God*, India, 2005

Below: *Tara*, India, 2005.

Symbols, India, 2005.

Above: *Religious Figures*, India, 2005.

Opposite: *Mourning Ceremony*, India, 2005.

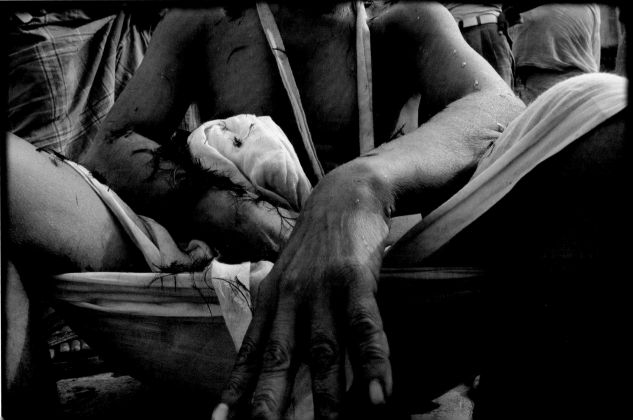

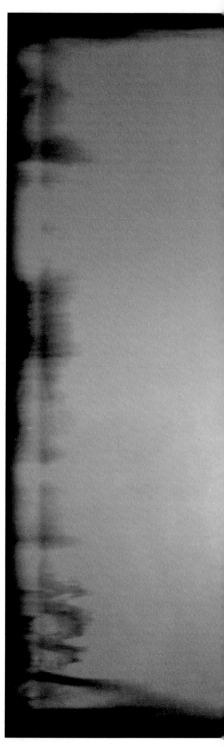

Guru, India, 2005.

Actress, India, 2005.

Goddesses, India, 2005.

Back Street, Calcutta, India, 2005.

ZoneZero Editorials

By Pedro Meyer

Family Album

[June 2000, www.zonezero.com]

N 1940, MY MOTHER TOOK this picture of me standing in front of my father, Ernesto, both of us with our hands in our pockets. The photograph had been in the family album for a long time; I recently rediscovered it. Today, in addition to my first son, Pablo, who is now inching towards 40, I have a second son, Julio, who is 5 years old. After seeing the picture in the album, I asked my wife, Trisha, to take a picture of Julio and me in the same identical pose as in the picture of my and my father, standing in the park in Mexico City.

Too many people associate computers and photography with the application of filters to an image, which in essence almost never adds anything but confusion to what, more often than not, ends up being a poor picture. Filters can be great tools, except when they are thrown at you with an "in your face" attitude, leaving nothing to imagination or creativity. In an era of instant food, and instant almost anything, there is this fantasy that one can also generate instant art—simply by clicking on the filter tool of choice, which alters the image into an incoherent, slapdash mess of displaced pixels. Clicking on an endless array of available filters in the absence of any critical thinking partly explains why nothing more interesting is likely to emerge from such a process.

In opposition to such mindless games, the computer allows us to explore countless new possibilities in the realm of the imagination, and in the exploration of time and place. For instance, take the seamless blending of past and present into new images, which deliver yet new meanings to those held individually by each portion of the whole.

The exercise of going through a family album and looking at the past is for many of us not an easy experience. In part it has to do with revisiting the images of loved ones who have passed away. In part it has to do with the memory of moments we sometimes would like to forget, or wonderful moments that have long been gone and which we miss. For one reason or the other, looking at old family pictures is usually an emotional experience. For this very same reason, there is the potential of coming up with very powerful new work derived from recycling past moments into new meanings.

The Meyers, 1940/2000.

Consider the image of "fathers and sons" that I have posted here. In this picture, I could very well be the father of my own father, as the age difference between us would allow for such a consideration. In that case, I would end up being my own grandfather, or for that matter, my little Julio's great-grandfather. But then there is also another possible configuration: that of Julio and I being brothers. Julio, upon looking at the picture, came up with yet another iteration, namely that the image had been taken by both his mother and by his father's mother. What we are contemplating in essence is the continuity of life between generations, only in this image the time line is not of the usual linear kind, due to my having had a child late in life. Such "cosmic confusion," as my friend E. Beardsley would call it, draws poignant attention to what our usual expectations are. Never before have we been able to make visual representations of such matters with such ease as today. Herein lies one of the more interesting fields of photographic exploration that I can think of.

In terms of psychology, I imagine that therapists could use this potent new combination: photography and computers. The act of changing and altering one's history through images—moving around and playing with the positioning of partners, parents, children, siblings, and so on—can no doubt offer new insights into our personal histories. From social sciences to the political landscape, such alterations can also allow us to revisit the past with new ideas and directions in light of the present. Blending the past and the present is more than the idle notion of cut and paste associated with the more linear time frames found in previous artistic expressions. Rather it is a more subtle and nuanced delivery of a layered consciousness; a new awareness of how we perceive facts and timelines, and of how we deal with our present in relation to past and future events.

A few days ago I was working on a video interview with two ex-Jesuits that I met about 30 years ago while photographing in a slum area in Mexico City. While talking with them, I noticed how time had been compressed; their history of three decades came down to a scant few hours of taping. One expressed a particularly poignant revelation: At the time, they all thought their efforts to help people in those slums was a failure. So much so that he, upon leaving the Jesuit order out of frustration, joined the guerrilla movement in Central America. That did nothing, either, as he saw it then, to improve the quality of life of the people he was fighting for. We sat talking in the same area that 30 years earlier did not have a single paved road, no electricity, water, or sewerage, no houses other than cardboard shacks. The interview was held in an apartment on the third floor of a very good building, however modest, where before there had been nothing but abject poverty. And we arrived at a new perspective: Indeed, a lot had been changing all along, and for the better, only no one had had the patience to consider the long run (30 years) to be an acceptable time frame for social change, and therefore it had progressed, for the most part, unnoticed. In the same way we are often unaware of day-to-day changes in our next of kin.

All of that is now open to new insights by looking at past and present within the same frame.

I strongly believe that if we continue to explore issues related to "time," and use photography and computers towards such a goal, we will discover an unending array of new threads to our present lives, and in the process create some exciting new images!

The Poetry of an Image

[September 2002, www.zonezero.com]

WE ARE TOLD (by the Encyclopedia Britannica) that "Poetry is the other way of using language." Yet when we make reference to other art forms, in our case specifically to photography, we seem to use the term *poetry* to describe a particular form of imagery. The other ones, I suppose, are considered to be equivalent to prose.

"Poetry," the Britannica also says, "is the way it is because it looks that way, and it looks that way because it sounds that way and vice versa." Here we are already bringing in formal elements, to give photography a more intimate connection with poetry as a language, and to help us look at photography.

Distinguishing poetry from prose—a perennial quarrel—is like distinguishing rain from snow: Everyone is reasonably capable of doing so, and yet some weather is either-neither. And so it was when I recently gave a lecture in Santiago de Chile, that I presented the image (right) of two men crossing in the background while in the foreground a woman was sitting at a counter, having some food, wearing two hats.

De Par en Par, Ecuador, 1985/2001.

For me there is poetry in the forms of this picture, the repetition of the elements in pairs, the two men, their legs taking similar steps in opposite symmetries, the woman with the two hats. There is a tendency of poetry to incremental repetition, variation, and the treatment of many matters and different themes in a single recurrent form such as couplet or stanza. Such thoughts animated me to put the image together such as you see here. Let me repeat, should the term have gone past you without further thought: I put this image together. Yes, I did so, digitally (see the pictures I used, at the end of this article).

After the lecture, I received an angry email from a young man who thoroughly rejected the notion that such an image had any merit once that I had commented about its digital origin. His particular objections were directed to the fact that I had not stood there, like a hunter of the "decisive moment," in the hope of capturing the two men in their corresponding strides, but rather taken the "easy way out" by implementing my ideas in the computer. He went on to complain that the poetry in this image was completely lost, as it could only have been achieved by way of the magical moment, that instant that things come together when the shutter is clicked.

I imagine that the author of that letter, whom I never met personally and I therefore have to assume combined the notions of a Zen archer with those of a photographer, assigned a particular importance to the essence of capturing the image "en vivo." For him that was the only poetic moment possible; he had no room for any other option.

Fair enough, I would say. However, our critic forgot to include in his equation that there are now other interesting Zen moments as well. Namely, those of sitting in front of a screen and honing your abilities to arrive at an image that did not exist before, or at least not in that state, and which is the main product of one's sensibility. The image does not come together on its own, you must make it happen. In that sense there is no distinction between composing images, music, or poetry. After all, one could also make a case that poetry is put together from words that were just lying around.

So, we can conclude that it's how you put together the notes for music, the words for poetry, or the images that were there before, that determines whether what you end up with is in fact poetry or just prose. Furthermore, we should also emphasize that photography is no longer solely what it used to be; it has been strongly transformed by all the digital options now available, and with that has come the obligation to rethink some long-held notions of what constitutes the photographic moment and where photographic poetry resides.

Ecuador, 1985.

Ecuador, 1985.

Revisiting Street Photography

[July 2003, www.zonezero.com]

FOUR YEARS AGO THIS MONTH, I wrote on the topic of street photography. At the time, I was disheartened with the problems related to making images on the street—both the security of the photographer or his equipment and the sheer refusal of so many people to be photographed. To make matters worse, there was also considerable lack of interest in this genre of photography on the part of galleries and publications. It also seemed that the number of photographers making pictures on the street had reduced, judging by the Portfolios section in ZoneZero—compared to the large quantity of street photography done in the past.

Out of a total of 480 portfolios published in Zone-Zero, only 49 have images one could consider as street photography. We have therefore decided to do something about this, by creating in the Portfolios area an entirely new section dedicated solely to street photography. Something which, looking back, we should have done four years ago.

I am glad to report that all is not lost, as some of us had felt. I have just been to Madrid, Spain, and my experience of photographing on the street

there contradicts entirely what I had stated back in 1999, and what many of you had come to believe as well. Not only did I feel safe photographing on the streets there, obviously taking the needed precautions one would take in any major city, but the people were inviting and totally at ease with the notion of having a camera pointed at them. Even photographing in the streets of Mexico City has become somewhat safer. Technological developments since 1999 have also introduced some interesting new variables. For instance, the more recent digital cameras have the ability to expand their ASA ratings much higher than previously possible, providing us with a very good degree of low-level light sensitivity while producing relatively little image noise. Then there are new filters for noise reduction, also contributing mightily to making low-level-light photography a very reasonable option. So the quality of the image has been considerably expanded. The speed and reaction time of digital cameras has also been significantly improved—something that is essential to street photography. You can hardly capture the quintessential "decisive moment," which is so closely linked to the style of street photography, if your camera is never ready when you need it.

Lavapies, Spain, 2003.

Today with higher sensitivity, higher quality of image information, and greater handling speed, we are ready to see a significant growth in this largely abandoned sector of photography. But the good news does not stop there. We have also found a plethora of potent new digital cameras that are very small and unobtrusive while retaining some of the traits of larger cameras, making the possibility of taking pictures on the street less of a security issue, as one can carry them in a pocket

and bring them out only when needed and under conditions that do not invite aggression.

As for the publication of street photography, some have complained there is no market for it and that galleries are not interested in showing it. Well, that's not entirely true. I have received numerous press releases about shows that are related to street photography. The possibility of printing these pictures in large formats is something that in the past also eluded most of us with traditional darkrooms. Now, with digital cameras, we can go to larger format printing, which is highly valued by galleries, at less expense.

In addition to the possibility of having your work seen throughout the gallery circuit, Web sites such as ZoneZero are bringing street photography to audiences worldwide in numbers that would have been only dreamed off in the past. No traditional gallery can offer the level of exposure for street photography that Web sites can provide.

We are at the threshold of great changes in photography, and as with everything else in the world, *adaptation* seems to be the driving force. Street photography has undergone a dark period for some years, and I believe that we are entering a new era in which this genre of photography will once again receive the attention it deserves.

However, there is one major issue to which I'm still giving thought: the notion of the "decisive moment." The more I come up against it, the more convinced I am that we have to move on and understand that all the attributes that have been attached to the so-called decisive moment are nothing but romantic ones. They pertain more than anything to an era that belongs to the birth of the 35mm camera. The assumption that we can actually see all the elements within the frame at the so-called decisive moment is a whole lot of nonsense. It does not serve well to educate photographers under such fictitious aspirations.

Although I am the author of the image shown here, I'd never claim to have seen all the wonderful things in it at the moment I clicked the shutter. There is no way I could have seen the simultaneous realities of all those visual planes operating in

parallel. Of course, one can argue the very Zen idea of perception: that I did not have to see it all in order to see it all; that I saw everything with my third eye; that I saw with my intuition, and so on. Well, fine,. Let us suppose this all could be true. But then why does this not happen every time I take a photograph? After all, my intentions are no different from one day to the other. If I have developed the skills that served me so well on day A, why would they elude me on days B, C, D, and so on?

In fact, I would say it has to do with luck, above all. Yes, you also have to have luck in finding and making good images. But how does one teach luck to students? You see what I mean? If artistic performance is to be measured largely by the contribution of luck, I think we are missing something very fundamental. The decisive moment is a flawed concept of image production, one that has done a lot of harm to a lot of photographers who have seen their efforts vanish into thin air, as they seldom were able to find the images that would stand up to such an unrealistic expectation—being able to see all the parts of an image within a fraction of a second, in order to make them all fit and coincide marvelously at the time of triggering the shutter. It just does not happen that way.

This notion of the decisive moment has also been one of those burdens that street photography has had to endure. Hopefully we will now make some inroads into reconsidering the possibilities that digital photography can offer us in creating images that might otherwise have eluded us. Some have described the process as a *magic* moment when all things come together without being seen. OK, I prefer a bit less magic and a lot more reliance on my abilities to use the tools as I need them, rather as they see fit to work by themselves. Maybe the good thing is that today we have the option to do it both ways.

Vanishing Evidence:
Photographing at Night in Mexico City

[December 2003, www.zonezero.com]

THE STORY I'M ABOUT TO TELL takes place at the crossroads of analog and digital photography, sex, accidents, and numerous unforeseen twists and turns.

I had just been surrounded by 15 police cars. Their red and blue lights flashed, blinking all over the landscape at 1:30 in the morning. Surrounding my car were no less than 80 policemen, some of them carrying heavy machine guns that made the Terminator look like, well, just a governor of California. I must say that, if it had not been quite so real, this scenario would have looked like something out of a bad movie.

I found myself in this situation because I was commissioned by one of our main museums in Mexico City to produce a body of work for a permanent exhibition to be shown during the next five years. I would photograph the activities that take place in the city from 8 p.m. to 6 a.m. The inducement to cover those hours proved twofold for me. Not only did I find what went on during those hours very challenging, but I also knew that taking pictures under poor lighting conditions, and with digital technology, would certainly be an interesting experience. Compared to what could be shot on conventional film, I have found that my digital cameras are much more responsive to low light. And now, having a new Nikon lens, supported by a vibration-reduction motor, I would be able to add three f-stops. The new technology would offer amazing results.

The police cars that surrounded Meyer and his colleagues the night the photographs accompanying this essay were taken, 2003.

Policeman surrounding the cars of Meyer and his colleagues, 2003.

However, I would have to confront one major problem. Going around the city during those hours of the night and in the rough neighborhoods I was to visit was not what anyone would consider a safe situation, either for myself or for my photographic equipment. I had no desire to be mugged or separated from my digital cameras. For this reason, I asked the museum director if the Mexico City police department would be able to provide two undercover agents who could offer me assistance and protection during the week I would be taking the photographs. The police department showed great understanding and straightaway offered to help me out because the project seemed quite interesting to them. I was thrilled.

The project would begin the next week; all the pieces were falling into place very neatly. Yet, for all the precautions I had taken, I was unequipped to deal with an unforeseen turn of events.

Just before the project got under way, I suffered a major accident right in my own studio. As I was setting up some sound equipment on the rear side of a G5 Mac that had just arrived, my foot got caught between some wires. I fell down, injuring my Achilles' heel, which now would have to be operated on. The ripped tendon would have to be stitched back together again. My foot was placed in a cast so I would not be able to move it or step on it. I was to be confined to a wheelchair for the next three months. This scenario did not seem promising at all for the type of photography I had planned.

However, after feeling sorry for myself for a couple of days, I decided I would not let the accident derail my project, so, I started to view the problem from a different perspective. I now knew that the images would have to be different from those I

Prostitute in the Downtown, Late at Night, 2003.

would have been able to shoot under normal conditions. I did not quite know what this meant, although I could imagine some of the probable images. I would have to rethink the angle and height from which I would be photographing, under these new circumstances. I could easily imagine that the dynamics of what could happen in any place I would visit would also have to change, because I'd be arriving in a wheelchair, surrounded by an entourage of people. Instead of being the unobserved photographer, I now had to accept that I would be the focus of attention anywhere I went. Thus, I would have to replan everything. Naturally, this transformed my initial ideas.

Taking into account that my activities would require new strategies, I invited various friends to join me in the realization of the project. To begin with, I asked one of my colleagues to take pictures of me while I photographed from my wheelchair. I asked another colleague to make sound recordings of the places we were to visit. Thus, we would

Pedro Meyer in a Wheelchair, Taking Pictures in a Night Club, 2003. Photo: © 2003 Enrique Villaseñor

later be able to create audiovisual material of this experience.

Other friends came along just for the fun of it and also to suggest places we could visit and in which I would be able to take photographs. Sometimes our entourage consisted of as many as seven people. As I could no longer drive, I had a chauffeur to drive my car who would also lend a hand pushing my wheelchair. Besides my own automobile, we were accompanied by another car, an unmarked police vehicle driven by one of the two cops assigned to protect both me and my equipment. The other policeman came along with me in my car.

Obviously, owing to the wheelchair and the amount of people surrounding me, every time we entered a place people would ask who I was. It wasn't hard for anybody to understand I had people protecting me. I suppose I must have seemed kind of enigmatic for most people: There I was, sitting on a wheelchair, several cameras hanging from my neck. My friends offered different explanations to the locals once they struck up a conversation with them.

According to each particular situation, they would say I was either a famous movie director looking for sets for his next movie, a politician who was enjoying a voyeuristic experience having a night out, or a TV journalist filming a story for one of the television networks. Paradoxically, the one and only thing I was never accused or suspected of being was a simple photographer—a fact which tells us something interesting about our profession and about how dull we are perceived to be.

The first night out, we tested the waters, driving around to see what sort of situations I, as a photographer, would be interested in capturing. As soon as I would see something that made sense to me, I would ask the driver to stop the car and have the wheelchair brought to me so I could get out and start taking pictures. It soon became clear to me that I was trying, in a very dysfunctional manner, to do that which I would have ordinarily done: get out of the car, and walk up to a situation that caught my eye. Only now, taking a picture seemed so cumbersome that I had to rethink everything.

I decided I had to come up with several new strategies so I could work more efficiently. One of my new plans was that, instead of getting out of the car myself, in the future I would allow someone in my crew to explore the possibility of my being allowed to take pictures at a particular location. As it turned out, at the first place I got out of the car I was forced to confront an entire team of threatening-looking kids who were bent on not letting me take any pictures at all—the fact that I was in a wheelchair made no difference to them.

Upon understanding the situation, the cops who accompanied me spoke to some of the menacing young men. And in less time that it takes to write this, these threatening young men changed their attitude and started to lift my wheelchair, making sure I would be raised onto a rather high sidewalk

Pedro Meyer Photographing at a Gay Disco, 2003.
Photo: © 2003 Enrique Villaseñor

and be able to move towards the store I wanted to photograph. Everything had suddenly changed, as if struck by a magic wand. I had no idea of what had happened; neither did I have a clue as to why on earth someone would object to my taking pictures there.

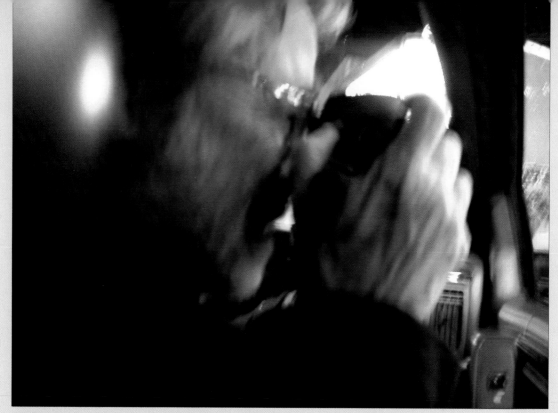

Pedro Meyer Taking Pictures from a Car, 2003. Photo: © 2003 Enrique Villaseñor

One of the cops later explained to me that the owners of the store, which sold Christmas ornaments wholesale, worked night and day catering to other vendors who, in turn, would sell their smuggled Chinese wares all over the city. The owners did not look upon my photographic endeavor as a cultural exercise, but rather as an effort to gather evidence against them. In one of those strange twists that continued to happen throughout the week, it would be the cops themselves—the ones accompanying and protecting me—who would make all the different people feel that they did not have to worry about my picture taking. I am sure the irony is not lost: The cops put their fears to rest, instead of making them dread the consequences that might result from evidence of their smuggled merchandise.

I discovered another strategy that seemed to make sense under the circumstances: It consisted of taking pictures from inside the car instead of getting out. The people in my entourage and I discussed a new issue that changed the designated driver of my car. My usual driver was no longer in charge of the vehicle during our nightly excursions; one of the two assigned policemen offered to become my driver, for he had been trained in surveillance techniques and knew how to drive the car in a way that would enable me to take pictures.

The scenes we encountered from the car were diverse—from prostitutes lighting up a small bonfire in order to warm their behinds in the bitter cold nights of Mexico City, to soldiers being arrested for urinating on the sidewalk, and people collecting discarded materials to make a living—all representing very basic human needs.

Street Scenes at Night, 2003.

Women at a Nightclub Waiting to be Asked to Dance, 2003.

The escapades went on nightly. We were politely turned down in many nightclubs, table-dance places as well as transvestite clubs. The main reasons we were given actually made sense: The managers wanted to protect their clients. They felt concerned that my pictures could compromise their clientele, because they didn't know if the pictures would eventually be published, even though I had the very best intentions in mind. The more elegant and upscale the establishment, the less amenable they were to letting me photograph. But not everyone turned us down.

In one of the beer halls we went to, we sensed trouble almost as soon as we got inside. The undercover cops came up to me and explained the exit strategy we would follow in case things got rougher. They would rush only me out of the place in my wheelchair, leaving the others to fend for themselves, the police explained; their assignment was to protect me and no one else. The trouble started when a lovers' brawl flared up between a transvestite and his/her lover. Beer bottles were thrown. The owner of the place was a fellow who, in spite of being a deaf mute, had a keen sense of all that was happening around him. He had strict control over his own people. His waiters knew exactly what he expected from each of them, one of them explained to our group. As soon as tempers flared, I was pulled out of the direct line of fire by my bodyguards. This was the opposite of what I wanted. I would have preferred to walk up to the

Cat Woman, 2003.

Men Fighting, 2003.

scene and taken shots of the whole ordeal. But I was in no position to do so. The men who had orders to protect me did not mess about with any other options. They just did what they had to.

Later, one of my friends told me that, as we were leaving the place, the people across the table from us seemed uncomfortable with us being there. Under their table they were passing each other the loot they had obviously taken in during that day: all sorts of watches and odd jewelry. I must admit I never saw any of that. From my vantage point, and with all the things I had to deal with, noticing such details escaped me, not only at that moment but at other moments as well. Sitting in

a wheelchair was evidently taking its toll on my photographic radar.

Taking pictures from the car started to work out quite nicely. The policeman who drove my automobile actually did have a sense of what I required as a photographer. This included the angle of vision, the speed in relation to subject matter, and last but not least, the issues concerning my personal security. This theme would become crucial in our next-to-last day of shooting.

One night we visited a gay club. There we met a group of friends who had gone partying that night, since the next day was a holiday. No sooner had I settled down and ordered a drink than I was run over by a beautiful young girl (who I later found out was an actress), and when I say "run over," I mean it literally. Although I had never met her, she sat on my lap as if we were old friends and began to crawl all over me.

She then told me to place my hand on her breast. My friend Rogelio (in the right-hand corner of the picture) expressed well the surprise we all felt. In fact, the photograph is an excellent example of how inefficient pictures are at conveying *the truth* many photographers search for so desperately. The image does not explain anything of what really went on. What's not seen in the photo is that the young actress's date or boyfriend was standing to the side telling her, "Come on... let's go," and she was probably trying to make him jealous. As so often happens, what lies outside of the frame is as important as what is within it.

The boyfriend's jealousy is also an assumption—I have no idea how truthful it is. Another possibility is that she was just attracted to a certain limelight, to seeing me arrive (she apparently knew who I was) with my crew of people. With the flash of cameras snapping perhaps she was prompted to become part of the "show" (after all, she is an actress). The truth is that nothing of this was more real than a film scene, a fiction that people believe in because it's supported by an image, a photograph by a photographer I don't even know—it

Meyer: "I was 'run over' by a young girl I had never met," 2003. Photos: © 2003 Enrique Villaseñor

simply appeared in my camera. Someone must have picked up the camera and simply snapped the moment. So, not only is the veracity of the content in the image suspect, but the author is unknown as well. However, if you want to imagine that I am a ladies' man, go ahead! Just remember, the evidence is only a photograph.

After this fleeting encounter, a young artist sat next to me and began to tell me about his career. He was a very nice young man who spoke to me with great pride about a tattoo he'd got recently and all the money he had saved so he could afford to have such a great piece of art etched into him. He offered to take his pants down to show it to me as soon as he realized that I would not be offended by him doing so. Then the conversation was interrupted by another young lady who introduced herself as a student of mine.

She said that if I wanted to photograph in the club, she would be glad to wheel me around the place. I agreed, and she pushed me around the aisles as if I was a kid sitting in one of those supermarket carts. Finally, she brought me onto the dance floor, left me sitting at a table, and had the waiter bring me a pitcher of beer. Before that, she took my wheelchair and drove me straight into the men's restroom—or she tried to—thinking that I would get some great images there. Instead, the wheelchair got stuck in the narrow entrance. My self-appointed guide explained to anyone who wanted to listen why she was pushing me into the men's toilet. She told them that I was a voyeur and that they should not worry. Not that there was anything to see, so I went along (what else could I do?) with the parody.

I was taken aback that everyone was so polite and friendly. There was no aggression in the air. I told

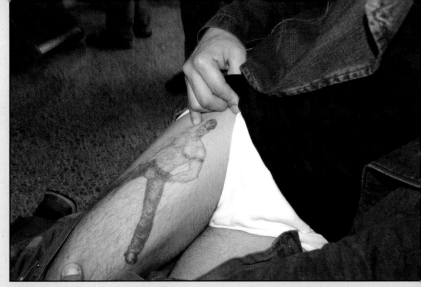

Meyer: "An artist showing me his tattoo. He saved money for a long time, he told me, so that he could afford to have the work done by an important tattoo artist," 2003.

Meyer: "This is one of my students, who I ran into at the Oasis, a gay bar," 2003.

one of my friends I had been to kids' parties where there was more tension and aggression than I perceived that night in the club. Thus I came across another myth about "those places" people are scared of going to.

Dancing at the Oasis, 2003.

Downtown Dance Hall, 2003.

Prostitutes on the Street I, 2003.

Street prostitution was one of the main topics I wanted to photograph, as it is a thriving activity in Mexico City. We headed towards several areas where you can find some of the more fanciful ladies of the night. I was hoping to catch glimmering images from the window of my car. There we were, driving along in our two-car convoy, just as we had on previous days. The people in the second car were coming along just for the ride, as we were planning to go someplace else afterwards.

I was taking pictures when, all of a sudden and out of nowhere, five characters started to pound on the window of my car, demanding that I turn over my camera. I just waved them off, while the cop driving my car suggested we better get out of there. It wasn't worth the hassle to confront them directly. So, he veered to the left with great expertise, speeding away into the traffic. We thought we had been able to evade the confrontation when two blocks down the street we were cut off by two cars. Out of these cars climbed the

same thugs who had threatened me earlier. They rushed towards us with the clear intention written all over their faces of breaking into the car and grabbing my photographic equipment. They began stomping and kicking the side door of the car. At this point, the cop driving my car flung his door open, pulled out his gun, and pointed it at the thugs while, very calmly, he began telling them to get the hell out of there. Meanwhile, the cop in the other car had made a special maneuver. He exited his car and was also pointing his gun at these characters from the other side.

Seeing themselves cornered, the thugs withdrew. All the members of my entourage—still sitting inside the two cars and watching the events— sighed with relief on seeing that nothing worse had happened. It could easily have turned into a shooting gallery worthy of a B movie. The cops got into the cars once the thugs left. We drove off, hoping this would be the end of it. But this was not to be.

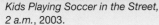
Kids Playing Soccer in the Street,
2 a.m., 2003.

Prostitutes on the Street II, 2003.

As it was, we were intercepted again a few blocks further on, only this time by patrol cars. At first there was one, then another and another, and soon we were surrounded by 15 units. It seemed strange to be stopped by the police, especially when the driver of my car was an on-duty policeman. So if anything, I felt intrigued as to what the next episode would hold in store for us. The night seemed to be filled with the pulsating lights projected by the turrets of all the police cars, with their red and blue lights streaming and bathing everything along their path.

Reinforcements came from all directions. It seemed as if they were preparing for an invasion. They carried machine guns of every caliber. They also had what seemed to be missile launchers, grenade launchers, and tear gas launchers. However, I did not see anyone with sniffer dogs trained for detecting drugs or explosives.

We all decided to remain calm within the safety of our vehicles. All of a sudden, the commander of all these police agents peered into our driver's window. He demanded our driver to identify himself and was taken aback when he discovered that now he had on his hands a far bigger headache than he had bargained for: The people he was pursuing were policemen themselves. Each of the policemen started to make calls on cell phones to their respective higher-ups, asking what they should do and how they should deal with the situation. Each of the patrol car units was ordered to cool down and to de-escalate the whole thing.

The main problem was that the Chief was obviously protecting the prostitution mafia. Thus, he could not so easily tell them to get lost and forget about the whole thing since by that moment they (the pimps, the five guys, and two women) had already arrived and were yelling at us with false accusations. So, the Chief discreetly whispered into

Meyer: "The woman is one of the matrons who deals with the prostitutes. She's standing next to a police captain," 2003.

our car: "At the very least, these people want you to hand over the roll of film you took." On hearing this, I explained, "I am sorry, there are no rolls of film in these cameras. These are digital cameras." I must admit that with great astuteness and candor, the police Chief responded: "Well, then, I will send one of my men to buy a roll of film someplace. I will then hand it to you, so you can pretend you are taking the roll of film out of your camera. Maybe we will be able to end this whole matter once I hand the roll of film over to them. All right?" I said: "That's fine with me."

While waiting in our cars, I observed the arrival of still more police units, reinforcements sent by the department to which our two undercover policemen belonged. They discreetly acknowledged each other, as no one was supposed to know they were actually allies. I began to learn about such matters as my companion in the car started revealing all these layers of information; I had no clue who

they were. He went on to tell me what they were planning to do: They would disarm the cop in the other vehicle and then bring his gun over to my car. The other cop's gun was handed through the window to the undercover policeman driving my automobile. He slid it down the side of his back while leaning backwards and handed the gun to me so I could hide it in my camera bag. I placed it at the bottom of my equipment, underneath all the cameras and lenses. Then the policeman who was driving my car took his own gun out of its holster and handed it over to me as well. I now had two guns, in addition to my own cameras and lenses. I only feared what would happen if one of these two guns went off unexpectedly while it was on my lap. I wondered if the shot would blow off my balls or my stomach.

The vanishing-evidence acts were going on all over the place, the newly arrived roll of film—all blank—stood in for the digital images on my memory discs. The hidden guns were now replaced with fictional stories in which no guns ever existed. I had become a government official whose bodyguards were abusing their powers, according to our accusers. The pimps, in turn, never even came close to bothering us in our car. The cops who came to help make the guns disappear were, in turn, acting out their part, pretending they didn't know the cops in my car. The cops who were protecting the prostitutes were supposedly just doing their duty—responding to charges brought by innocent civilians. Not a single person told the truth about anything. By now, even I was lying, saying I did not know anything about any guns.

As I sat there, I could not help thinking of all those stupid debates around the "truth" surrounding photography. I was wondering, how in the midst of such a sea of lies, anyone could dare to take a picture and offer it as a representation of the "truth." Bush and his make-believe Thanksgiving turkey in Iraq, also came to my mind.

The mafia wanted blood, but by now there were no guns to be found anywhere. Police officers came swarming down upon us and started to inspect both cars. They checked underneath the seats and also under the car as I sat there, camera bag on my lap. I looked on nonchalantly.

The Chief suddenly eyed the bag and asked, "What's inside?"

"My cameras and all the different lenses. Would you like to see?" I said while beginning to remove most of the equipment. He felt satisfied with the quick search.

Meyer: "These cops are surrounding our car," 2003.

Meyer: "A television crew heard that we'd been surrounded by the police, and they arrived to interview us," 2003.

I asked one of my two undercover agents to explain why on earth, if what they were doing was legal, they needed to hide their guns. He explained that the most important thing under the circumstances was not to let the issue escalate further, because it could slowly develop into a legal and political embarrassment for some senior officers. So, the more one could do to defuse it, the better. No sooner was that said than we had TV cameras and their lights streaming through the windows of our two cars. There were also radio reporters and people from the Commission on Human Rights coming to defend us. After all, with all the bells and whistles that must have gone off on one of the main thoroughfares of the city, it was just a matter of time before the press arrived in full regalia to find out what was going on.

At this point, I had had enough. It was now way past five in the morning. So when the press reporters came, and the people from the Human Rights commission made their appearance, I explained to them the full story. After all, I had every right to take pictures from my car, given that I was on a public street, not on private property. Also, I was taking photographs for a museum and I had all the credentials to prove it. Besides, the two policemen protecting me were on active duty. So, bearing all this in mind, I prompted the Human Rights people to please ask the women, who were still yelling at the top of their lungs, if they truly felt they had any complaints pending against me. By now, they had all realized I wasn't the high government official they imagined me to be and from whom they could extort some sort of benefit. So, with incredible politeness, they waved me off (they had now discovered I was in a wheelchair) saying they had nothing against me. I should leave. "But those two cops and that other guy," (meaning my personal driver, who had been sitting in the other car, and who had gotten out of it with his cell phone in hand, and who was now mistakenly being accused of allegedly holding a gun instead of the cell phone), "they will all have to be taken to the police station to stand charges," the women and the Human Rights people demanded.

I said, "Fine. Get one of my friends to drive the other car and another one to drive mine." (Remember, I was unable to drive myself.) "Please let us depart as soon as possible." What I was really thinking was that the guns in my camera bag had to leave the place as soon as possible. And so we drove off.

No sooner had we arrived home, than I received a phone call from the police station. The woman who had wanted to press charges against us was willing not to do so if we paid her 3,000 pesos (approximately $300 U.S.). She explained that this was the cost of the medical bills she would have to pay in order to overcome the grief she had had to endure, as she now had these terrible pains in her chest. I said yes, and the two undercover cops and my driver were able to leave the police station straightaway, without being booked.

What I did not know at that moment—one of the cops explained this to me later—was that all this was settled so fast and easily because the officer in charge of writing the complaint realized that they did not have any guns or cars as evidence.

He asked the plaintiffs, "So, if you don't have the cars, are you going to tell me these people arrived by foot?"

Well, without the cars and without the guns as evidence, the situation seemed quite ludicrous and hilarious.

For me and the people who accompanied me that fateful evening it was a night full of very interesting issues concerning our different perceptions. In fact, it all had to do with each person's assumptions and beliefs. It was a dance of distorted fields of reality and vanishing evidence.

Meyer: "This was one of my bodyguards, Arturo. He put on these fun glasses and we joked about him being a secret agent," 2003.

Does Size Matter?

[January 2004, www.zonezero.com]

HAVE YOU EVER LOOKED at your email inbox to find several messages with the subject head, "Does Size Matter?" I think you might have. I read somewhere that about 250 billion of such spam emails have been sent all over the world.

This past winter, in Vol. 30 of *Camerawork*, the prestigious journal of photographic arts published in San Francisco, I came across an interesting article by Geoffrey Batchen entitled, "Does Size Matter?" Batchen's article made reference to the intimacy between the viewer and the size of the photograph; he questioned whether the size of the image affected the viewer's experience of the photograph.

Oddly, it turns out that in his well-documented article the existence of the Internet as a source for viewing photographs is totally ignored. It would seem, according to the examples presented by the author, that the only public places one can look at pictures are museums or galleries.

Strangely enough, even Seydou Keita from Mali, one of the photographers Mr. Batchen mentions in relation to the sizes of images Keita exhibited in the recent past, is a photographer whose work we've featured on the ZoneZero Web site for the past six years, yet Batchen seems not to be cognizant of this fact any more than he is of the Internet in general. I am sure that if he had included the pictures exhibited on the Web when considering the impact of image size, his analysis would have benefited.

Batchen states, "Of course putting a big photograph on a wall doesn't in itself preclude the viewer from a potentially intimate experience of it. But it doesn't help either. Photography places all its subjects firmly in the past and this temporal distancing is repeated by larger photographs in spatial terms, literally pushing us back from the print as well as from those subjects. But going miniature is not necessarily the answer either, for intimacy is not quite the same as physical closeness (you can have sex with someone and not be intimate with them). The problem here is that intimacy remains a hard thing to define. You know it when you feel it—that sense of personal, private involvement with another person or thing, of a shared emotional investment in that relationship—but it

Walking Billboard, New York City, 1987/1993.

remains a nebulous, not-quite-describable kind of experience often measured at the level of the body (in the gut) rather than the intelligence."

(I take exception to this assertion that photography places all its subjects firmly in the past. In the early part of the 20th century, Albert Einstein saw through nature's Newtonian facade and revealed that the passage of time depends on circumstance and environment. He showed that the wristwatches worn by two individuals moving relative to one another, or experiencing different gravitational fields, tick off time at different rates. The passage of time, according to Einstein, is in the mind of the beholder. I wonder: Which watch's photograph would be in the future relative to the other one?)

If one considers that on the ZoneZero Web site we receive more than two million page views per month (mostly with one image per page) the number of images that are being reviewed in this manner is high enough that a serious writer simply can not ignore such viewing habits. So when the author of "Does Size Matter?" uses such a title without so much as a colluding wink, one gets the impression that he probably doesn't "get it" when it comes to experiences outside the realm of his spaces of reference. The reasonable statement about intimacy mentioned above is most certainly shared by an ever-increasing number of people who are populating the Internet, otherwise the exponential growth we have experienced would have never taken place.

If the issue is the dissemination of images, no museum or gallery can compete with what is available on the Internet, not even remotely. As such, the Internet is already the largest museum in history. And according to my friend Chip Simone, it is probably the best thing that has happened to museums and galleries since the Medici family.

Interestingly, Batchen's only references to large-scale prints are images presented in museum or gallery spaces, such as those by Andreas Gursky, Richard Avedon, Thomas Ruff, and Cindy Sherman, yet somehow the large-scale pictures delivered via billboard advertisements (such as those seen in Times Square, on the Sunset Strip, in Piccadilly Circus, or on the Ginza), or those that appear on large cinema screens, are simply ignored in the article, just as the Internet is ignored. It's as if the influence of photographic culture coming from these corners of the world does not figure into the decision-making process regarding the size of photographic prints. Nor is any mention made of the fact that the size of prints has increased because today we can print extremely large images with much the same ease that we used to print an 11 × 14 inch.

In the past, I could not dream of printing at the sizes I print today; my darkroom was just not large enough to accomplish such a task—neither the room itself nor the chemical trays would accommodate making a print that was, say, 44 inches wide. For most of my life as a photographer, I never printed larger than 11 × 14, because the papers were all too expensive and I did not have the facilities to make larger prints, facilities that are readily available today through digital technology. Digital technology is also the reason that I, and many other photographers, are now working primarily in color. We were limited in the past by the technical complications, all of which have been superseded in the digital age. With the ink-jet printers available today, you can accomplish whatever your imagination leads you to do. In the past, it wasn't possible for me to work in color with the same ease that I worked in black and white, much as I tried.

What I find so amusing today is that collectors are suddenly jumping on the bandwagon of buying up "vintage" silver-based prints, discovering all of a sudden that the prints photographers made in the past, which were often put down as not being a unique artistic product, were just that all along. Prints which, not long ago, could have been bought for a few hundred dollars are today selling for ten to twenty thousand dollars, because there were never more than a few printed, due to the scarcity of materials and the photographers' limited time. I had always maintained we had a built-in constraint in our potential to produce large numbers of prints, but then the idea did not take hold.

In conclusion, I don't know if size matters, but facts do, and I am constantly reminded how facts are often ignored—either by those who write about photography or those who collect images, and they ignore them to their own detriment.

As I was writing these last sentences, my inbox rang and I received an email with information that to some degree I had been expecting for a long time: Kodak was announcing that it had stopped selling traditional film-based cameras. I suppose the impact of such news will have serious repercussions all over the photographic world as people will now, inevitably, have to come to terms with the facts we have been discussing here in ZoneZero for years.

Sonora, 1981.

Next page, left: *Michoacan*, 1981.
Next page, right: *Tuxtla Gutierrez, Chiapas*, 1982. **191**

Aguascalientes, 1981.

Tuxtla Gutierrez, Chiapas, 1982. **197**

198   *Tuxtla Gutierrez, Chiapas, 1982.*

Aguascalientes, 1981.

Aguascalientes, 1981.   **201**

Chihuahua, 1981.

Colima, 1981.

Guadalajara, Jalisco, 1981.

Developing Pictures

By Pedro Meyer

South Africa

Color enhancement done with photo software brings out the elements of light in a picture because it can be done selectively, and with far greater levels of control than can be achieved in a traditional film-based darkroom.

Comparing the gray-looking landscape picture [1] to the sun-lit image [2], it's easy to see that the color controls largely determine the mood of the photograph. Interestingly, the colors were embedded within the picture itself—they were not added by extra-photographic means.

The woman was taken from another picture—this one [3], in which she's seen surrounded by friends—and inserted into the landscape, making sure that the color scheme of one image worked with the color scheme in the other.

One also has to make sure that the cultural context of one image works with the image it is being associated with [4]. For instance, in the case of this picture, employing that particular South African landscape makes sense given that the woman is from the region.

1

2

3

Todos Somos Palomas

It would be nearly impossible to get all the elements in these three photographs [1–3] together in one plane of a picture using traditional analog photography. Consider how many shots you would have to make to have all the birds and the man in the top hat converge in a harmonious way, in focus, and in the right proportions. The probability of that happening is exceedingly slim.

I propose, then, that the ability of the photographer be determined by his creativity in the service of his ideas and feelings [4], rather than the presence of sheer luck, such as a camera shutter clicked at an opportune moment.

1

2

3

4

Cuba

When I visited Trinidad, Cuba, in 1980, the Cubans were building housing projects for farmers, like the structure seen in the background of this picture [1].

At about the time I took the picture of the farmer in front of the building where he lived, I also made a photo of the entrance to one of the haciendas or plantations where such a man might work [2].

It is common to make a link between what you've seen in one place and what you've seen in another to create mental pictures of people in the places they're connected to. Now, for the first time, we can easily make such associations photographically, in order to tell a story with a single image that, in the past, would have required several pictures [3].

❶

❷

The Meyers

Two men and two children: The man on the right is my father, and the kid in front of him is me . The man on the left is also me, and in front of me is my son, Julio [1], when he was roughly the same age as I am in the picture of me and my father.

Because of the difference in ages between my father and me in the original photos [2 and 3], I could have been my father's father in the composite image [1], in other words, my own grandfather. Or I could be my father's brother, my own uncle.

In the past, such cosmic games were the province of poets, writers, and film directors, but hardly the territory of a photographer anchored in reality. Now, with the advent of digital cameras and software, photography is on a par with other art forms. Photographers can make a visual statement such as this one without possessing near-impossible technological prowess.

2

3

Senora de los Pollos

I often work with differences of scale within the photographic image, which is something that digital photography lends itself to. In the case of this picture, the beggar woman [1] requesting support from passersby is presented in front of an altar to the Virgin of Guadalupe, which is surrounded by dead chickens [2].

For me, there is a strong connection between the dead chicken [3] as a metaphor for sacrifice and the iconic representation of the religious altar and the beggar woman. I associate these elements with the manipulation of sentiments.

What is so interesting to me is the potential that photography has acquired in this digital era to use a single photographic image [4] to express an idea that, in the past, would have more likely been dealt with in another way—painting or collage, for example. I like the ease with which I can make a complex editorial statement within a single image.

❷

❶

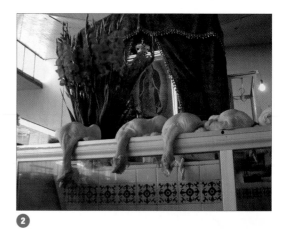
❸

④

Free Film!

It all started with an image I shot on the street of a man offering "Free Kodak Film." I took the statement to mean *free* as in *freedom*. In other words, "Liberate Kodak film." [1–2]

I was on my way to an opening of a Richard Avedon exhibition in New York, where I took pictures of the Avedon images hanging on the wall [3].

Upon looking at the style of the Avedon pictures, the thought came to me that I could give the street image I'd shot an Avedon-like aesthetic—now that I had the option of working with the image on a computer. So I gave my photo a white background and black surrounding frame [4], just as Avedon would have done had he taken the image in his studio.

①

②

③

④

I then placed my photograph alongside one of Avedon's images as if it were part of the exhibition. I also took some bees from the man in Avedon's photograph (*Ronald Fischer, Beekeeper. Davis, California, May 9, 1981*) and placed them on the face of the man who was liberating Kodak film [5].

As there were some people in the photo I took of the Avedon exhibit, it occurred to me that, thanks to digital photography, I could take a picture I'd made of the man with the sandwich board and place him within the gallery, as if he were visiting the exhibition himself [6–7].

In one picture the man on the street is a picture hanging on the wall. In another he's a spectator. It is strange what the image of a person within a photograph does. It's always a matter of context.

6

5

7

Bangladesh

I found the gaze of this street vendor both mysterious and sad [1]. I wondered if he was tired, or perhaps upset with me for taking pictures. I don't believe it was the latter as everyone I came across in Bangladesh seemed to relish being photographed. Here was a gaze I did not understand; I couldn't read the man's emotions in the photo I took of him.

①

During lunch, at the center where I was to give a lecture, I took a picture of a mural painted by children [2]. Later, it occurred to me that the colors and the forms of the mural would make a lively background for the image of the man with the indecipherable gaze.

I didn't intend for this combination to have any particular meaning. It was a purely aesthetic choice, but one that again brings up the interesting juxtaposition a photographer imposes when he places someone before a backdrop—even a white one [3], such as Avedon used—that alters the photo viewer's perception of the place the subject was standing at the time the picture was made, which is a way of manipulating the viewer's perception of the subject [4].

In the new postclick environment, it's important to be aware that many of our traditional ways of thinking about photographs must be reconsid-

③

②

ered and revisited. Given that we can now easily modify a photographic image after it's taken, we need to better understand and cope with the conceptual implications. For generations people have been used to thinking of the photographic image in a linear way, believing that the documentary nature of the picture was maintained as long as any manipulations of the image took place before the camera's shutter was triggered.

The South Park Street Cemetery

When I travel, I usually visit cemeteries to get a glimpse of the local culture with regard to that most universal of experiences: death. The grandeur with which British colonialism presented itself everywhere was part of what I imagined I might also encounter at the Britsh graveyard in Kolkota (Calcutta), and I was not disappointed.

However, though I pointed my 35mm-format digital camera in every direction, I felt I could not adequately capture the unique atmosphere of the place. By making several shots [1–3] and later splicing them together in the computer [4], I believe I produced a better representation of what that eerie park looked and felt like when I was there.

❶

2

3

4

ZoneZero Editorials

By Pedro Meyer

The Icons of This War

[May 2004, www.zonezero.com]

DON'T THINK IT'S too farfetched to assume that the main icons of this still-in-process second U.S. war in Iraq will be the amateur digital pictures of the tortures performed on detainees at Baghdad's Abu Ghraib prison.

In spite of the tens of thousands of pictures produced by professional photographers during this war, these amateur images are the ones that I believe will mark this period in history. These will be emblematic, not only for the abuse performed on the physical integrity of the human beings depicted in them, but the pictures will also stand in for the shame many feel for allowing themselves to be swayed in providing support for this unnecessary war. The use of systematic disinformation (remember the weapons of mass destruction?) and torture will likely become the downfall of this administration. It will then have turned out to be that digital cameras were for the Bush administration what the tape recorder was for the Nixon White House.

The images that stand out, at least in my imagination, of the first war in Iraq, are those that CNN broadcast live, with night-vision lenses that gave a green cast to the scene, showing how Baghdad was being bombarded. Back then CNN was still in the news business, whereas today they appear to be more in the advertising business. You can tell that their loyalty is no longer to the news but to their advertisers whom they try not to alienate, much in the style of Disney, by presenting information that is free of controversy. The levels of disinformation by the U.S. news media are almost as appalling as those of the U.S. government.

I participated in a Congress on Photojournalism in Lima, Peru, last week, and one of the speakers was Cristóbal Bouroncle, the head of Agence France-Press (AFP) in Baghdad, who shared with us some very interesting information about the news business at his agency.

He mentioned that today the accountants are just as important in the decision-making process as the news editors. In other words, decisions made in the newsroom must weigh budget concerns on an equal basis with newsworthiness. In many ways this makes a lot of sense as the operation is, after all, a business. However, one should also wonder, why are profits the driving decision maker rather than the news? Of course that is something we shall never find out.

Bouroncle also explained to us that Western professional journalists are hard to come by, in the context of Iraq, because the security risks are so high, while local photographers are doing a very good job as they have access that Westerners do not enjoy, among many other reasons: language and belonging to certain tribal groups.

Bouroncle also noted that the locals get paid far less than Western photojournalists, which is a big plus with the accountants. And last but not least, thanks to the ease of using digital cameras, they are able to send out people to take pictures who are new to photography and have had minimal training. These novices come back with very good imagery. Interestingly enough, among other very revealing bits of information, Bouroncle estimated that roughly 50 percent of the AFP pictures taken in Iraq are used by Internet news outlets rather than print news media.

If the most emblematic images from this war were photographed by amateurs, if agencies can send out virtually untrained photographers, and if we are seeing a tidal wave of imagery coming from all the digital cameras that are flooding the world, I'm certain that traditional photojournalism as it's now being taught in schools all over the world better have a second look at reality. The photojournalism traditionalists should be prepared to tell their students that things are no longer how

they used to be and they must therefore adjust their expectations.

The same thing might also prove to be of interest to all those active photojournalists today who are seeing their bread-and-butter documentary images being displaced by pictures of celebrities and movie stars.

What Was That About Originals?

[July 2004, www.zonezero.com]

MY COLOMBIAN FRIEND, Juan Alberto Gaviria, and I were in Brazil recently. At a local gas station store I came upon a cardboard-cutout image of one of Brazil's supermodels promoting a brand of beer. It reminded me of another image I took 16 years ago in Los Angeles, of a cardboard cutout depicting then-President Reagan. I was intrigued at that Brazilian gas station by the strong visual effect the representation of a cardboard woman had on the person who was being photographed next to it.

Juan Alberto, ever the gentleman, was proving to be enormously tender, almost not touching the model, even though the image was nothing other than cardboard. In contrast to the strong hug given to the girl by the man in the Reagan picture, in both instances, we are of course just looking at surrogate realities.

This form of projecting ourselves onto images is very much what happens in the cinema, where our subjective self is intermingled with the images seen on the screen. We feel like hugging the actress of our dreams in much the same way.

I might add that the intervening years between the two images brought forth a new element to such work, namely the use of color; something that was made possible for those of us who started to work with digital cameras. Before, when I used film, I could only afford to produce work in black and white. Today, most of my colleagues who used to work in black and white, and who now use digital cameras, have also moved from black and white to color.

But going back to the issue of representation, let us look at the picture taken in the cathedral in Brasilia, which I visited recently. You will find there a reproduction of the *Pieta* by Michelangelo (the original of which is in Rome), and the Holy Shroud (the original of which is in Turin). The latter is a framed enlargement of an X-ray image (already a further level of abstraction), and what do people do when viewing this image in Brasilia? They take pictures of themselves in front of it, and also in front of the *Pieta* reproduction. For them apparently there is no difference or need to differentiate between the original and the copies.

Brasilia, Brazil, 2004.

Cardboard, Malibu, California, 1988.

The Venetian Hotel, Las Vegas, 2001.

The Venetian Hotel, Las Vegas, 2001.

Come to think of it, there is not that much of a difference for all those who go to Las Vegas and have their pictures taken in front of every sort of reproduction that one can find there.

What's more, many of the reproductions in Las Vegas are not even the reproduction of an "original" but of yet another reproduction, which only through the patina of time became itself an "original." That's the case, for instance, with the Campanile in the Main Piazza de San Marcos in Venice, which was itself a reconstruction. Therefore, the tower at the Venetian Hotel in Las Vegas is a reconstruction of the reconstruction that is in Venice. An original no longer exists. (See http://europeforvisitors.com/venice/articles/campanile_di_san_marco.htm)

Also, you'll find that the canals of Venice reproduced in Las Vegas happen to be flowing as you stand on the fourth floor of a building, with fake facades all along the sides. Everyone is quite content as they hear fake gondoliers sing out in well-intentioned, but artificial-sounding Italian accents.

But what is the difference, when President Bush makes a trip to visit the U.S. troops in Iraq for Thanksgiving only to pose with a fake turkey for a fake dinner, which he never really attended as he flew in and out as fast as he could. Or Bush's earlier faked landing on the aircraft carrier, dressed up in a pilot's suit in order to say, "Mission accomplished"? People want to believe their president and therefore suspend any critical judgment

Cathedral in Brasilia, Brazil, 2004.

Réplica do Medalhão
encontrado por
Constantino Xavier e
Ana Rosa

Trindade, Brazil, 2004.

in spite of the blatant deception that is behind all these actions.

In Brasilia, thousands of people lined up to pass in front of an altar, one by one, with a clearly marked sign indicating that the object of their veneration was in fact a replica.

Nonetheless, the multitude that had come from throughout the entire region, an area that was easily 300,000 strong, gathered in the city of Trindade in the state of Goias in Brazil, and found no problem bringing their devotion and money to the coffers of the church, which was very forthright in telling its devotees that what they had to venerate was a reproduction. All these good people had come for their annual "Romeria Do Divino Pai Eterno," which is celebrated on the first Sunday of July of each year.

We are left to question the moralistic approach that so many photographers have taken towards the representation of the image in these digital times, in so far as pictures "telling the truth." The central question: "What is the truth that is being told through images?"

Trindade, Brazil, 2004.

I believe it is helpful to take a look at how the world actually likes to see itself represented, and how far human nature is capable of bridging one's own reality with that of the multitude of representations that have nothing to do with being "honest."

There probably isn't a single "official" picture of a celebrity or movie star that is not doctored to make the person appear according to some fantasy of what he or she would like to look like.

For issues related to faith there is no possible evidence that is more real than the desire to believe—be that in terms of religious practices or in other aspects of daily living. The stuff dreams and desires are made of breaches all possible factual evidence that could run contrary to their intentions. How else can one explain the worldwide complacency in dealing with surrogate realities as if they were originals?

For example, take this religious Jew who, with his cell phone in his hand, is bringing someone's prayers to be "heard" by the Wailing Wall, otherwise known as the Western Wall in Jerusalem. It's a surrogate reality leap of major proportions. The need to be in front of the original wall is no longer a requisite, apparently.

When I first exhibited this image of the chair standing on a pedestal in the street, everyone who saw it was convinced that I had placed the chair there using Photoshop. The possibility that this would be a real chair was immediately dismissed. The more plausible explanation of a digital manipulation made more sense than the extravagant idea that in Washington, D.C., there is in fact such a chair. The notion of the real and the fake had come full circle. We now tend to dismiss the real because it looks like a fake.

The "truth" is that in their own way all fakes and surrogates become their own sort of original.

Monumental Chair, Washington, D.C., 1989.

A Photograph Is a Photograph
Is a Photograph

[October 2004, www.zonezero.com]

IN RECENT YEARS a growing number of those who use photographs in their work have started to shy away from describing themselves as photographers. They are now "artists," as if photographers were a different species than artists.

Well, to a degree they are, by what one can glean from the market it seems that if you consider yourself an artist, the same work can fetch considerably higher prices than if you are simply a photographer.

So, I don't know whether to congratulate such colleagues for their practical approach or to question their opportunism for being willing to dance to the tune of whatever the taskmaster demands.

But aside from any issues that might come across as moralistic in nature in this market-oriented environment, there seems to be something most everyone is missing out on. Let us take a closer look.

Photography is not what it used to be. A lot of people have tried to invent new words for the work that has been coming out in this digital

age; apparently we needed to coin new words to describe the work because *photography* was no longer an appropriate term.

Not only has there been an exodus of photographers to the land of the "artists," but on top of it, everyone is attempting to find new terms to describe the images produced in this age of computers. It appears that approval and major recognition is bestowed on the artist, not the photographer; obviously, economic favor follows. And if you can slap the label of *New* on something, it will probably also create more interest. That is what the market tells us.

Maybe this can help us understand the increased distancing from the terms *photographer* and *photography*, which have apparently become associated with old-fashioned, outmoded ideas.

However, I believe they got it all wrong. We should make every effort, especially at this point in the brief history of photography, to seize the opportunity to actually expand the horizons of photography, not abandon it, and not lose sight of where we can move on our own terms. I find that

Portrait I, Brazil, 2004.

Portrait II, Brazil, 2004.

photography is at the threshold of its greatest creative moment and the best times are yet to come. However, the nature of what we understood as photography in the analog age has to be reconsidered. Yes, photography it is still all that it was, but it's also a lot more.

The word *photography* means "writing with light." Well, never in my lifetime have I had a more direct experience of actually writing with light as I have in recent years, when using a stylus pen to move around, at my will, all those pixels that were captured through my digital camera or scanned from film.

To sit there in front of my computer screen, and to manipulate those pixels, has been the most direct experience I have ever had with the notion of what photography was always intended to be—at least from the standpoint of those who made up the word.

Today, I can explore and submerge myself to the very bottom of a sea of pixels, and touch each individual pixel through the pressure of my finger on a stylus, with no parallel to what could be done previously to the individual grains in a sea of gelatin with silver halides. This basic premise transforms all of photography forever.

With this new set of rules, the limits of photography are defined by our imagination. We can either expand our understanding of what photography is in order to broaden the field, thus making it a stronger and more influential player called *PHOTOGRAPHY*, or we can let things stand as they are and merely watch as it all slowly erodes. Photographs will then come to be called by another name, and no one will want to be identified as a photographer any longer. We either reinvent photography, by broadening what is understood as a photograph, or we may well end up not having much of photography to defend.

I for one find that the more I alter my images, the more photographic they become, but I am also looking at photography differently. I am convinced that as soon as we view photography with a wider perspective, the market will understand that there aren't so many dilemmas in this matter between being a photographer or an artist.

The strictest of documentary photographers will, to their great surprise, probably discover that, as before, there is room for a lot of such work under the term *photography*. After all, both poets and journalists use words, but what they do with them is quite different. Why should the photograph be considered any different than the word? In either instance every one understands the context.

However, having said that, we also call the poet a poet and not a journalist, which is probably why the slow migration of photographers towards the self-definition of *artists* helps us understand that such separations indeed define different working strategies that are distinctive and should not be confused. But we should all still be able to call a photograph a photograph. After all, paraphrasing Gertrude Stein, "A photograph is a photograph is a photograph."

Left: *Ramon Ali*, Brazil, 2004.
Below: *Les Murray*, Brazil, 2004.

What Is the Meaning of One Fish?

[December 2004, www.zonezero.com]

I DON'T KNOW THE STORY of this single fish, other than that it seemed to be quite important to these men at the fish market in old Dhaka, Bangladesh. I do not speak Bangla, so there was no way of finding out the context. This is of course the beauty and the limitation of photography: an image is open to any interpretation we wish. So, rather than speculate endlessly about the real meaning behind what we are looking at in this picture, I have decided to define its meaning for myself. It's about notions on the significance of wealth. How rich is a man with one fish?

Bangladesh is, according to economists, one of the poorest countries in the world. And of course the wages paid—about one dollar a day for breaking stones, or two dollars a day for pulling a rickshaw all day long with a huge weight many times larger than the individual doing the pulling—goes a long way in confirming that the announced levels of poverty in Bangladesh are no exaggeration.

However, statistics also tend to obscure other aspects of life that get lost in descriptions such as "among the poorest in the world." I found that the people in Bangladesh are among the friendliest I have ever met anyplace; not to mention that they must be the biggest enthusiasts of having their pictures taken on the face of the earth.

I did not find a single instance of someone not wanting their picture taken. What's more, I had a hard time making any pictures, as no sooner did I point my camera than I would find myself surrounded by dozens of eager candidates who wanted their image to become part of the intended photograph. To capture some degree of spontaneity I had to act really fast. That is, before the entire crowd moved in and wanted to join the picture.

I have no desire to romanticize poverty, nor to turn away from the reality of the Bangladeshis' hard existence. Yet it is also very narrow minded to just look at poverty in comparison to any Western standard of living. How does one factor in to such evaluations the ability of the Bangladeshi people to get along with each other, which is considerably better than what you typically find in the West? When my little son was in his first years in school, he was taught what was called

What is the Meaning of One Fish? Bangladesh, 2004.

Rickshaw Driver, Bangladesh, 2005.

"conflict management." The kids had to learn how to resolve conflicts, which is of course part of daily living. Those skills seemed to be something that needed to be taught in school. Here in Bangladesh, I have the impression that this is something they acquire in the water they drink. Their attitude about dealing with conflict in a positive manner is so widespread, surely they did not get such skills in a school program.

Here's a case in point: When there is a collision between a rickshaw and another moving vehicle, the first topic they deal with is how they can fix the problem, not who is to blame. In almost all of the West, the first thing is establishing blame. Obviously in a society of have-nots, resolving the problem at hand is more beneficial than fixing the blame—from the latter there is nothing much to be gained. In the West, the economic pursuit behind establishing who is at fault is the more important matter.

The issue of how people look at pictures took on another twist when I heard a story by Shahidul Alam, the man responsible for Chobi Mela III, (in Bangla, *Chobi* means *photo*, and *Mela* means *festival*) and the reason I find myself here in Dhaka.

Some time ago, during an exhibition that was organized here, a workshop was conducted and the students' work was displayed and presented to the community where the images were taken. One of the girls in the audience brought her goat to the exhibition, because she and the goat were in one of the pictures, and she wanted to have the goat view the picture. I doubt that in most of the West, the notion of bringing a goat to a photographic exhibition to see its image would occur to us. There are indeed many things that one can

Right: *Tiger*, Bangladesh, 2005.
Below: *Stone Crushers*, Bangladesh, 2005.

learn here where there are so many different ways of looking at photography.

Chobi Mela III is one of the largest events of its kind in Asia, bringing photographers and their work to the forefront during the festival's two-week run. I have met photographers from all over the region here, and I am sure that as this festival grows in coming years, Bangladesh will increasingly become a major center for the development of photography. And what better place to have such an event than in a city where photography is so widely welcomed by the population?

Here again, the often-mentioned statement that poverty and digital technology are incompatible is

brought to a screeching halt. I was able to print an entire exhibition here in Dhaka, with Epson providing the printers and papers, and it all worked perfectly well. Rather than shipping prints and frames all over the world and going through all the usual problems of customs and the inherent costs of shipping and crating, we circumvented it all by printing the show on site. The frames were all made in 48 hours—and what beautiful frames, on top of it all—and the exhibition opened on time. Another exhibition, sent from the United States, which was going to go up parallel to mine, never made it through customs.

I have written many times previously about safety and street photography [see "Vanishing Evidence:

© 2004 Shahidul Alam.

© 2004 Shahidul Alam.

Photographing at Night in Mexico City," page 167]. Well, here in Dhaka, as in any other large metropolitan conglomerate, there must be a number of "bad characters." Fortunately I have not run into them, or I do not attract them; either way, my point is that I would never dare run around Mexico City with the same degree of confidence that I feel here.

I am not the only one who feels comfortable walking the streets with cameras around my neck in old Dhaka. There was one photographer, however, from Malaysia, who seemed to run into trouble every time he went out. So, the question is, does one attract such problems while photographing on the street? Are some photographers trouble magnets because of their behavior? I wonder, and if so, I suspect that dealing with cultural differences is one of the things that needs to be included in photography school programs the world over. I do not know of a single school anywhere

that teaches such important matters to photographers. It is assumed that we know how to deal with such matters, and the truth is we do not.

As the year comes to a close, I am invaded by a degree of sadness, not only for all the great photographers who are no longer with us, who died during this past year, but also about the political winds that seemed to have prevailed against all odds, at least for the short run. Yet in spite of all of this, what keeps our spirits high is that creators of art throughout the entire world seem to be on the upswing. The intensity and dedication of artists throughout the world (yes, I view photographers as artists and artists as photographers, when they use photography) is thriving in spite of material limitations that appear to be part of the global landscape. It appears that having only one little fish is not such a terrible alternative when you know what to do and what to say. I get the feeling that there are more and more photographers who clearly understand this.

It's Reality That Astounds These Days

[March, 2005, www.zonezero.com]

WE ARE REMINDED by writer Nicholas Rombes that "today the real has become the new avant-garde." The irony is that as digital technologies are used to deliver ever-greater special effects and fantasies, there is an alternative tendency to use digital video cameras not to transform reality into some special effect, but rather to describe the world with increased realism.

In a sense, as Mr. Rombes points out, the new aesthetics—evident in recent movies shot with digital cameras, such as *Ten* (2002, directed by Abbas Kiarostami), *Tape* (2001, directed by Richard Linklater), *Time Code* (2000, directed by Mike Figgis), and *Russian Ark* (2002, directed by Aleksandr Sokurov)—rely on a species of strict formalism (the long take, the divided frame, etc.) to remind us that reality is the most experimental form of all.

Russian Ark constitutes an elaborate, continuous 96-minute take, the camera moving through Russia's Hermitage Museum—which is only possible to achieve with digital cameras, since no film-based camera could run for such a long period without having to reload. *Time Code* is a series of four separate 97-minute-long takes simultaneously shown in four quadrants. *Ten* is completely shot (without the director present) with digital cameras mounted on the dashboard of a car as it is driven through the streets of Teheran. And *Tape* takes place entirely in one hotel room. In a sense, the special effect that links these digital films together is reality itself; these films are considered experimental or avant-garde simply because they lack the jump-cut, speed ramp, freeze frame, CGI aesthetics that now form mass cultural media, ranging from television commercials, to music videos, to video games, to television shows, to mainstream movies.

When watching the *Lord of the Rings* trilogy with me, my 9-year-old-son, Julio, leaned over and asked if all those people were real, as we were looking at one of those scenes with thousands of marching warriors. Twenty years ago we would have been amazed to learn that indeed they were special effects. Today we are amazed to learn that such a crowd is, in fact, real.

Byzantine Saint, Bangladesh, 2005.

As I have been traveling around the world these past months, what has astounded me is how universal the trend has been to view the world through the eyes of digital technologies. But these technologies are understood for their special effects and not at all for the possibilities they offer us to view the real—in new ways.

We live in an increasingly fictionalized world. On the one hand we have politicians of every stripe, all over the planet, delivering the most preposterous manipulations of reality with words and images (they call them photo ops); and on the other hand we have the conglomerates of news media, from print to television, also on a worldwide basis, contributing in no small way to the fictionalizing of reality—to the extent that news events are sometimes so deliberately distorted or dramatized that one has a hard time figuring out what was real.

However, just as in cinema, digital technologies are helping to bring new forms to the medium of still photography. Photographers who no longer need to cater to the demands of the news media conglomerates, and their dictates of what can and cannot be presented to the public, are starting to find new venues to show their work. In that sense the Internet has allowed many such filters to be lifted; thus we can deliver information as close to the facts as possible.

In keeping with reality, after more than a decade of not needing to ever go back into the darkroom to make a print, I decided to finally pack up all my darkroom equipment and place it in storage for my great-great-grandchildren, so that one day they can look at those strange things we once used to make photographs.

Although I am not nostalgic in the least, I must say that taking all those items and packing them away was not so easy. After all, many of those things have been with me for decades. Now, ask me if I regret getting rid of these objects, and I must say, "Not for a small second!" I am totally delighted to be able to move on and live in the digital age, forever after. During this past decade, not once was I even tempted to step back into the darkroom. There is just too much fun to be had in the "light room."

As I was putting all my darkroom equipment in storage, I was also packing away all the envelopes of photographic paper. Among the names on those envelopes was Ilford. In a peculiar twist of circumstances, this week Ilford was in the news because the firm is being bought out by its employees, to see if it they can salvage it from financial ruin. Not long ago, Hasselblad had to restructure itself after going through a financial crisis of its own, while Polaroid was auctioned off some time back, and Kodak, the once dominant name in photography the world over, now has a market value that is but a fraction of Apple Computer's, a firm that did not even exist in Kodak's days of glory. And now get the news that Leitz, the manufacturers of Leica cameras, is also experiencing extreme difficulties as its strategy to enter the digital market has had one failure after another. Meanwhile, Sinar, the Swiss camera maker, cannot seem to sell enough of its studio cameras and is transforming itself into a distribution company. And lastly, one of the oldest brands in photography—Contax, which has produced cameras since the early 1930s, when the brand was launched by the optical legend Zeizz Ikon—has now joined the ranks of those who have had to close factories; Contax has suspended all production of both its analog and digital cameras, as the company apparently can't cope with the changes in the market brought about by digital technology.

Yet in spite of all this mounting evidence that there is simply no way back and that analog photography is nothing more than a mere period in the history of photography, and that we are going in one new direction only: digital—and as you see all these stalwarts of analog photography come tumbling down—you will wonder how on earth is it possible that anyone could still doubt the direction that photography is headed? Yet, believe it or not, that is what is still going on. I am sure the irony will not escape you, that those who dismiss with great passion what is happening today, place themselves squarely in the midst of "photographic realism." It's reality that astounds these days.

Index

Rio de Janeiro, Brazil, 2005.

These portraits are of some of the 300,000 people present at the
procession of the 2004 "Romeria do Pai Eterno," a celebration
that takes place each year on the first Sunday in July, in the city of
Trindade, state of Goias, Brazil.

Trindade, Brazil, 2004.

Trindade, Brazil, 2004.

Trindade, Brazil, 2004.

Trindade, Brazil, 2004.

Trindade, Brazil, 2004.

Rio de Janeiro, Brazil, 2005.